The Workbook

HELLO THERE!

Welcome to your workbook for **Susie Moore's "Let It Be Easy - Simple Ways to Stop Stressing & Start Living!"**

I'm Annie Agerbek, and I've created this workbook to help you get the most out of Susie's fantastic book.

We all know the feeling of finishing a great book and wanting to make changes, but sometimes it's tough to put those ideas into action. I've seen how powerful a book can be when you really dive into its lessons. That's why I've designed this workbook to be a helpful companion to "Let It Be Easy."

This isn't a standalone guide—it's meant to work with the book. Think of it as a tool to help you better understand and apply Susie's ideas to your life.

I hope you find this workbook useful and that it helps you turn Susie's insights into real, positive changes. Thanks for picking it up, and happy exploring!

Best,
Annie Agerbek

Table of Contents

- 00 Introduction
- 00 My Journal
- 01 Nature is Proof That Ease Surrounds Us
- 02 Add to Your Plate
- 03 Volume Creates Victory
- 04 The Best and Fastest Way to Change Someone
- 05 You Are Bigger Than What's Making You Anxious
- 06 Living Your Dreams Can Start Right This Second
- 07 If Something Feels Off, It Probably Is
- 08 It's Okay to Be Sad after Making the Right Decision
- 09 What to Remember When You Mess Up
- 10 Call Your To-Do List Your "Get-To-Do" List
- 11 Ordinary Routines Create Extraordinary Results
- 12 Wear Out, Don't Rust Out, Baby
- 13 Communications Without Confusion
- 14 You Don't Have to Defend Yourself, Ever
- 15 Success Is Very Unsexy
- 16 Drifting Off Your Life's Course Happens Slowly
- 17 "Best Thing I Never Had" is the Best Beyonce Song
- 18 Take Yourself Out to Lunch

Table of Contents

19   What to Know When You're Not Someone's Cup of Tea
20   Stop trying to balance everything
21   Everyone has invisible scars
22   See the world in high definition
23   A little extra makes all the difference
24   Be easy about sex
25   Argue for your possibilities
26   Just decide
27   Know your blind spots
28   Confidence is simply a willingness to feel uncomfortable
29   The past does not create the present
30   Desire is the greatest force in human nature
31   Grief is love
32   Every silver lining has a cloud, and that's okay
33   Let people know you're happy to see them
34   The next time someone gives you a weird look
35   Good and bad, you'll get used to it
36   If you don't feel like an imposter, are you really going for it?
37   If they gossip to you, they'll gossip about you
38   Call on your imaginary mentors
39   Stop saying I'm proud of you

Table of Contents

40	The best coaching question ever
41	The grass is greener because it's fake
42	Stop picturing success and do this instead
43	When you thrive, everyone wins
44	The next time someone gives you a weird look
45	Good and bad, you'll get used to it
46	Commitment Makes Life Easy - The 100% Rule
47	Loving You is the Real You
48	When You Think You're Not [Fill-in-the-Blank] Enough
49	The Best Thoughts Ignite This One Feeling
50	What Palm Trees Teach Us About Resilience
51	What You're Not Changing, You're Choosing
52	Fun is Always an Option, Even When Things Go Wrong
53	Don't Rob Yourself of New Experiences
54	We Are Everything We See and Feel
55	The World Will Always Match Your Energy
56	Saving Money is Expensive Sometimes
57	Just Be On Time
58	Don't Underestimate Your Contribution
59	Boredom is Dangerous
60	It's All Relative

Table of Contents

61   No One Intends to Screw Up Their Life
62   Good Enough Is
63   Tell People Who Are Suffering They're Not Alone
64   Couples Therapy: Just Do It
65   Unmute Yourself
66   The Present Moment Creates the Past
67   Don't Deprive Others of the Joy of Helping You
68   Putting Yourself First is Generous
69   A Secret Superpower
70   Don't Just Consume, Create
71   Talk About It Already
72   Stop Fighting With Yourself
73   Australian Wisdom You Can Use Every Day
74   Success Leaves Clues
75   How to Give the Perfect Gift
76   You Spot It, You Got It
77   A Positive Mental Attitude Can Save a Life
78   Your Value Is Not Determined by How Other People Treat You
79   Someone's Death Does Not Define Their Life
80   It's Okay to Break Up with a Friend
81   Let's Revel in Your Accomplishments for a Second

Table of Contents

- 82 Can't Forgive? That's Understandable
- 83 There's No Such Thing as Normal
- 84 Take a Stand for the "And"
- 85 The biggest manifesting magnetizer: Appreciation.
- 86 Keep Your Network Alive
- 87 Pity is Never Helpful
- 88 Divorce is Not a Big Deal
- 89 The Secret to Contentment - Even if you feel lonely or sad or lost
- 90 Sulking is Worse Than Fighting
- 91 Just 30 Minutes is Enough
- 92 Don't Give Up Hope on a Strained Family Relationship
- 93 The Pickup Line That Resulted in Two Husbands
- 94 Give People Quantity Time
- 95 Priority is Meant to Be Singular
- 96 The Pursuit of Happiness is Miserable
- 97 Drop the Ball Sometimes
- 98 It's Better to Be Happy Than Right
- 99 Anticipatory Fear Is the Worst Kind of Fear
- 100 Putting Yourself Down Is Exhausting for Others
- 101 The Core of Any Phobia Is loss of Control
- 102 Actions Have Consequences

Table of Contents

103   Ask yourself, how much of my life was my idea?
104   Use Perspective to Relax
105   Victims Need Villains
106   Never Say, "I Don't Have Time"
107   Humans Are Wired for Mimicry
108   Take It Seriously, but Hold It Lightly
109   Be Generous in order to Win
110   Give the People You Love Permission to Die
111   Desire Requires Distance Sometimes
112   Unused Talents May as Well Not Exist
113   Happiness Is a Short Memory
114   When in Doubt, Zoom Out
115   Deflate Drama with Distraction
116   Say Sorry First
117   Build Trust with Yourself
118   People Who Don't Trust Can't Be Trusted
119   Know Your One Thing
120   See the Child in Everyone
121   Love Is What Makes a Family
122   Four Words to Be Wary Of Using
123   When You Want to Give Up, Remember This

Table of Contents

124 Live and Let Live: The Ultimate Wisdom
125 Nostalgia is Dangerous
126 Too Late is a Decision, Not a Position
127 Raise Your Hand Even When You Don't Know the Answer
128 There's Nothing Uncool About Practice
129 Find Commonalities with Your "Enemies"
130 Let Selling Be Easy
131 Be Flexible When Unexpected Things Happen
132 One Day, You Won't Even Be a File in a Hospital
133 Replace Your Knife with an Axe
134 Batch Your Life!
135 The best way to make a friend
136 Only Action Cures Fear
137 You're Apologizing Too Much
138 Qualifications Aren't Everything
139 Closure Requires Only One Person
140 You Don't Have to Finish What You Start
141 What You Don't Like in Someone Else, You Probably Don't Like in Yourself
142 Doing It Is Easier Than Not Doing It
143 Be a Light for Others
♥ Review

Introdution

In the introduction to "Let it be Easy" by Susie Moore, the author reflects on a pivotal moment in her life when her marriage was on the brink of collapse. She shares how her need for control and constant criticism pushed her husband, Heath, to the edge, leading her to seek therapy as a last resort. Through therapy, Susie realized that her stress and need for control were the real issues, not her external circumstances.

Her therapist helped her see that she had been unknowingly addicted to the stress she created in her life. Despite having read numerous self-help books, Susie hadn't fully grasped the importance of letting go and allowing ease into her life. This revelation was both shocking and liberating for her. She understood that if she was the source of her problems, she could also be the solution.

Susie emphasizes that the idea of making life easier isn't about denying real pain or challenges but about changing our response to them. She suggests that many of us hold the unexamined belief that life must be hard and that good things come only through struggle. By questioning this belief and choosing to see life through a lens of ease, we can transform our experiences.

The introduction sets the stage for the book's main premise: life can be easier if we allow it to be. Susie shares her journey of learning to let go, relax, and embrace a more gentle and compassionate approach to life. She invites readers to explore this philosophy and offers practical, real-life strategies for letting ease in, ultimately leading to a more fulfilling and joyful existence.

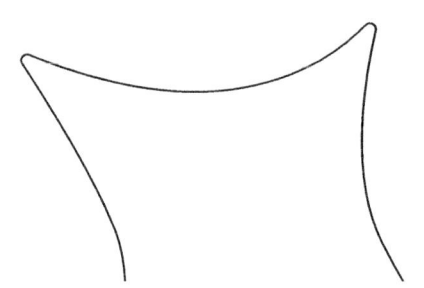

Journal

WHAT WAS EASY FOR ME WHEN I WAS A CHILD?

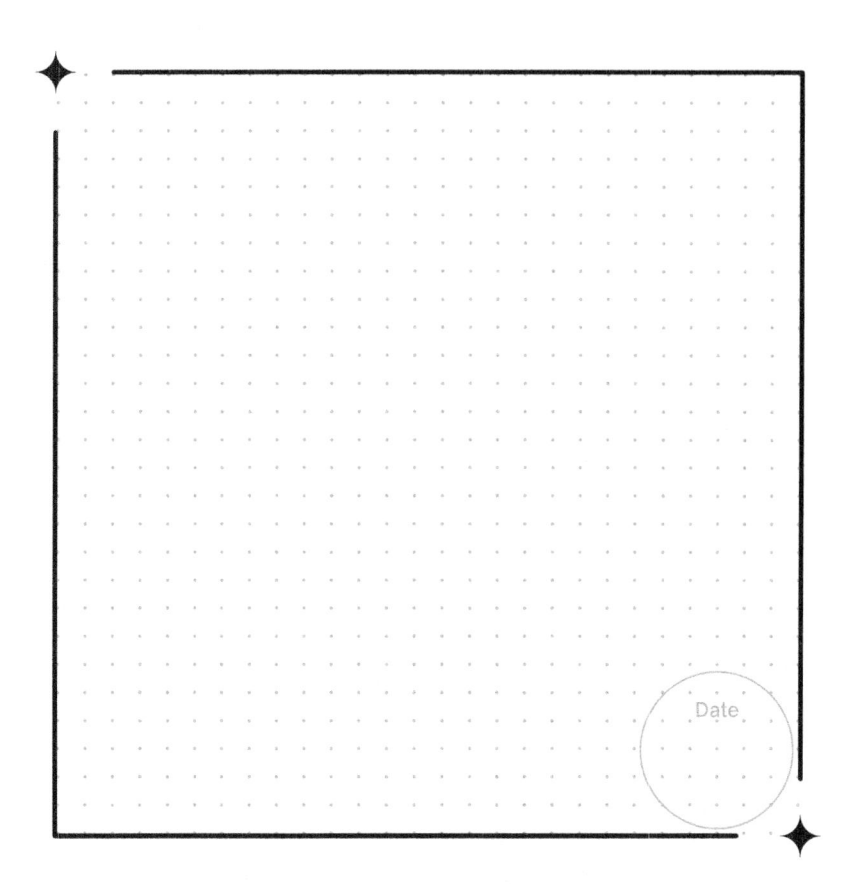

Date

Journal

WHAT SITUATIONS OR AREAS OF MY LIFE DO I FEEL THE MOST STRESSED OR ANXIOUS ABOUT?

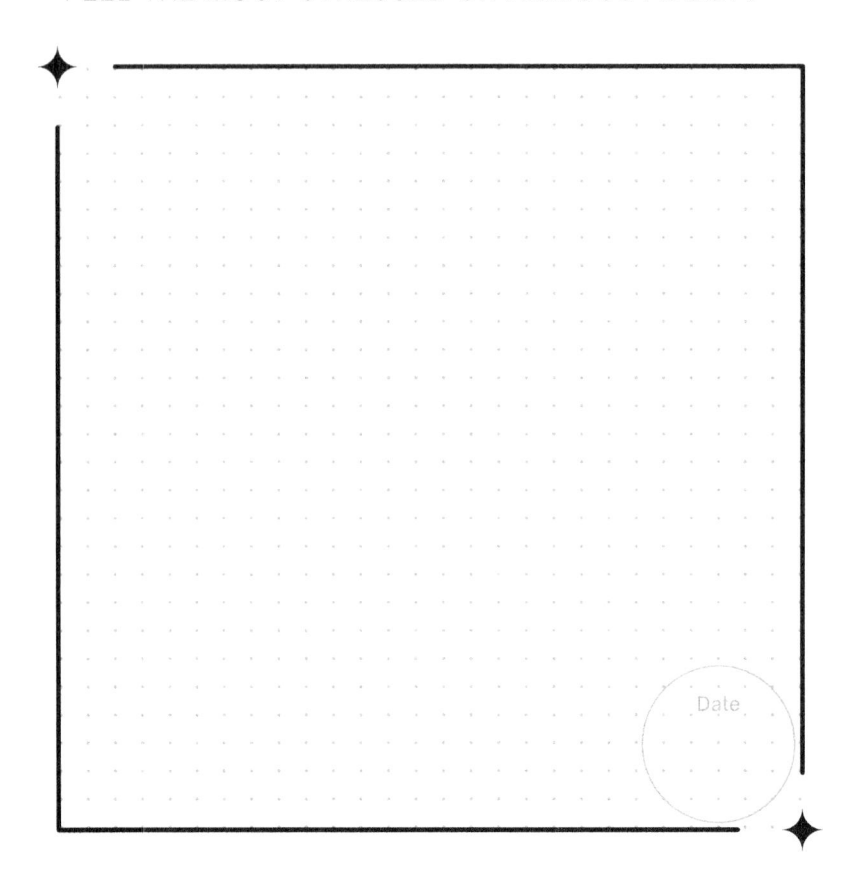

Date

Journal

IN WHICH AREAS OF MY LIFE DO I WISH FOR MORE EASE?

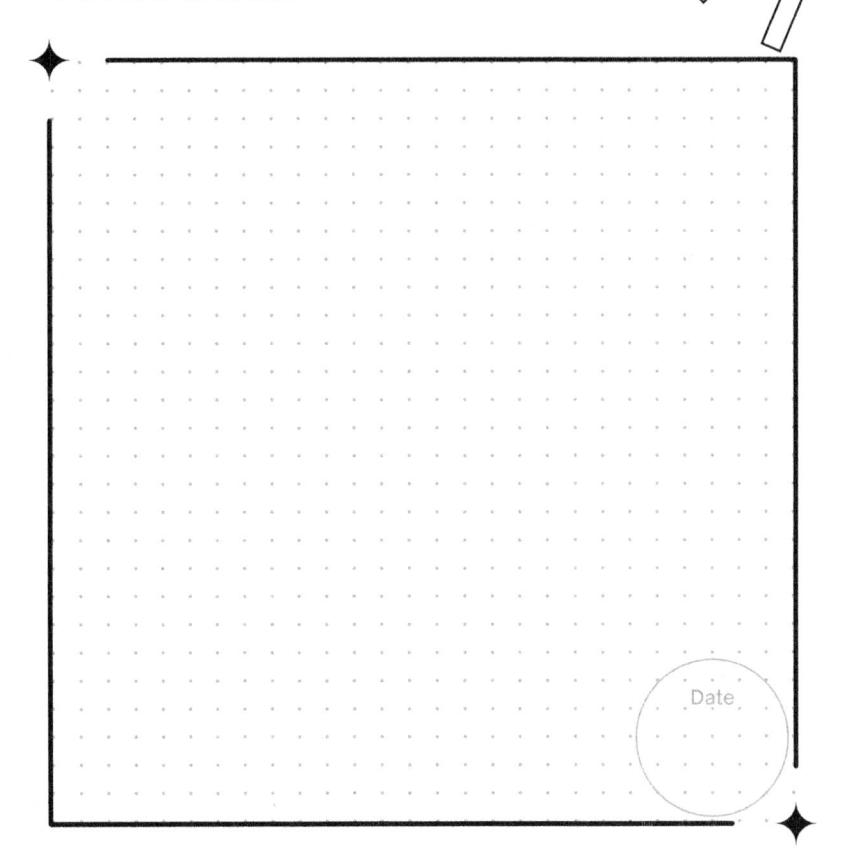

Date

Chapter 1

NATURE IS PROOF THAT EASE SURROUNDS US

- **Embrace Simplicity:** Using fresh, in-season ingredients with simple additions like olive oil, lemon juice, and salt can create extraordinary meals, illustrating the power of simplicity.
- **Avoid Overcomplication:** Many people unnecessarily complicate tasks, believing they must be difficult to be valuable, but this mindset often prevents them from even starting.
- **Nature's Abundance:** Nature provides flexible, abundant solutions that can make our lives easier, showing that embracing ease can lead to joy and success.

MY KEY TAKE AWAY

"

Date

"

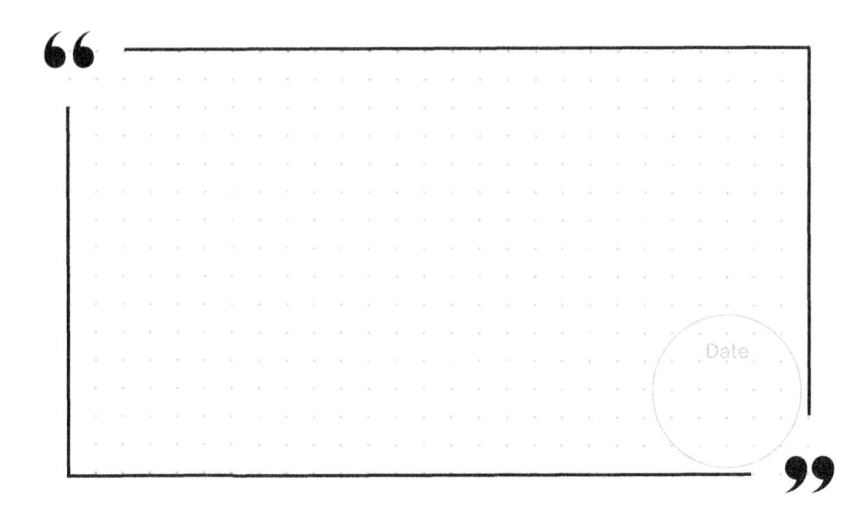

Journal

IS THERE AN AREA OF MY LIFE WHERE I AM OVERCOMPLICATING SOMETHING THAT WANTS TO BE EASY?

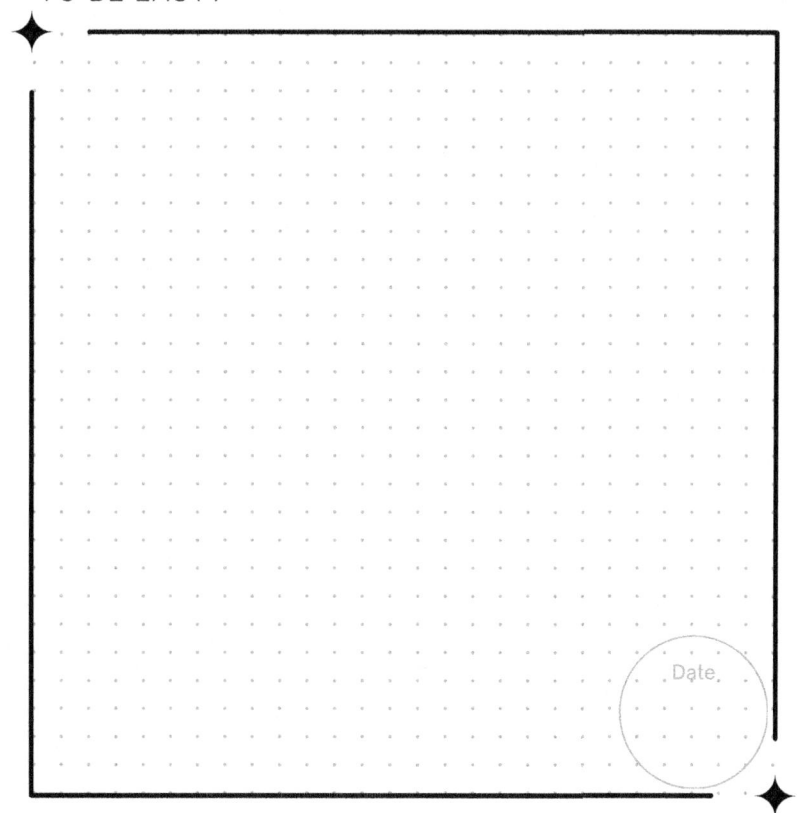

Date

Chapter 2

ADD TO YOUR PLATE

- **Crowd Out Negativity:** Just as a health coach fills a plate with colorful, nutritious vegetables to crowd out less healthy options, we can improve our lives by adding positive influences and experiences.
- **Expand Your Horizons:** By seeking out new people, activities, and communities, we can naturally displace negative elements and enhance our overall happiness without focusing on what's lacking.
- **Variety and Openness:** Embracing a variety of experiences and options can prevent us from becoming overly dependent on one source of joy or fulfillment, making us more resilient and satisfied.

MY KEY TAKE AWAY

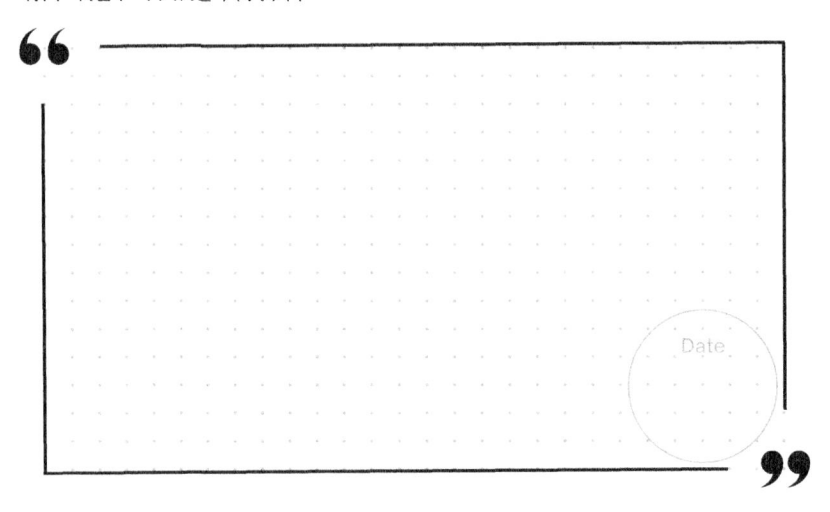

Date

Journal

HOW CAN I ADD MORE POSITIVE AND FULFILLING ELEMENTS TO MY LIFE TO CREATE A MORE BALANCED AND JOYFUL "PLATE"?

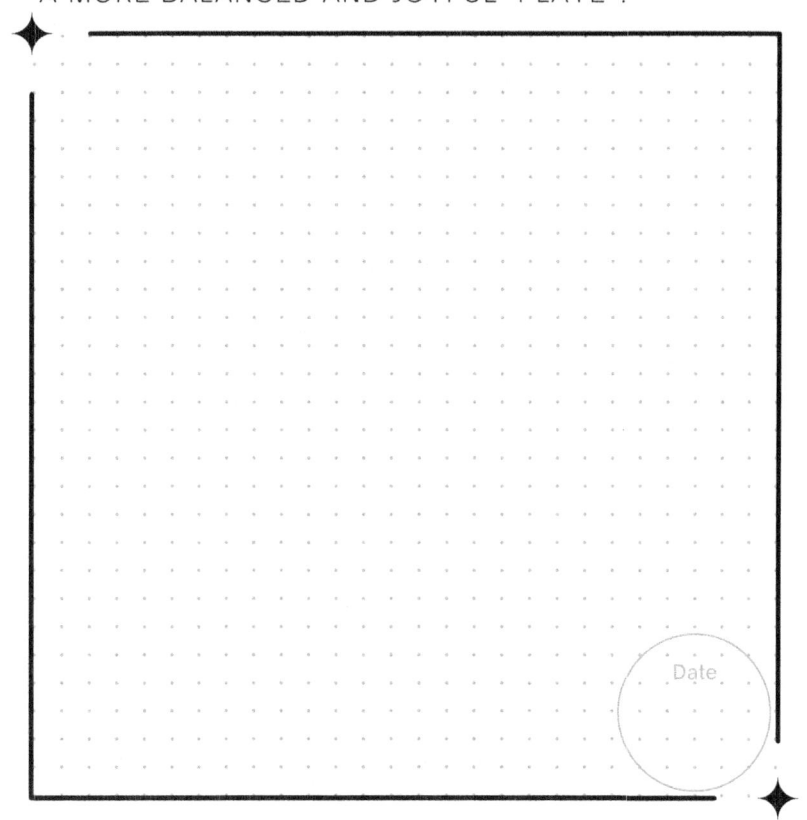

Date

Chapter 3

VOLUME CREATES VICTORY

- **Action Leads to Success:** High achievers like J-Lo, Dolly Parton, and Daymond John succeed not by doing one thing perfectly, but by consistently creating and taking action, learning from failures, and moving forward.
- **Embrace Failure:** Failures are part of the journey to success and are often hidden from public view. Successful people don't dwell on failures; they use them as stepping stones and keep pushing ahead.
- **Consistency Over Perfection:** Success comes from continuous effort and volume. It's not about achieving perfection in one attempt but about the accumulation of efforts and persistence over time.

MY KEY TAKE AWAY

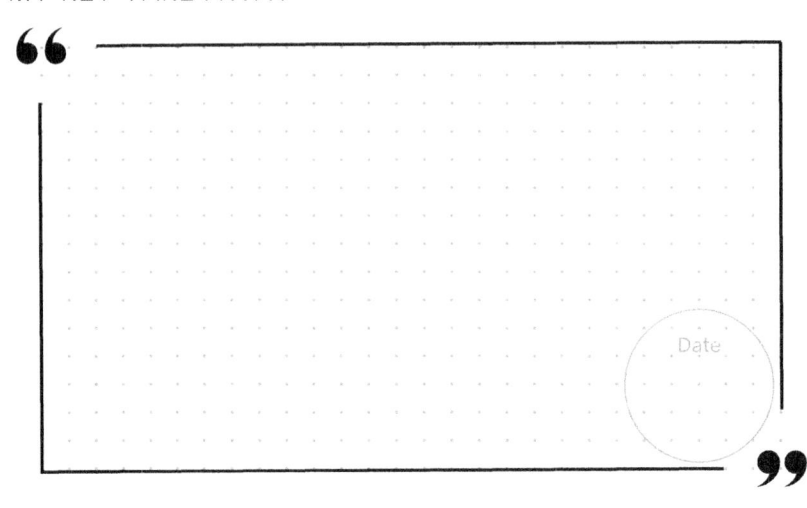

Date

Journal

HOW CAN I INCREASE MY VOLUME OF EFFORTS IN PURSUING MY GOALS, AND HOW CAN I REFRAME MY FAILURES AS VALUABLE LEARNING EXPERIENCES TO KEEP MOVING FORWARD?

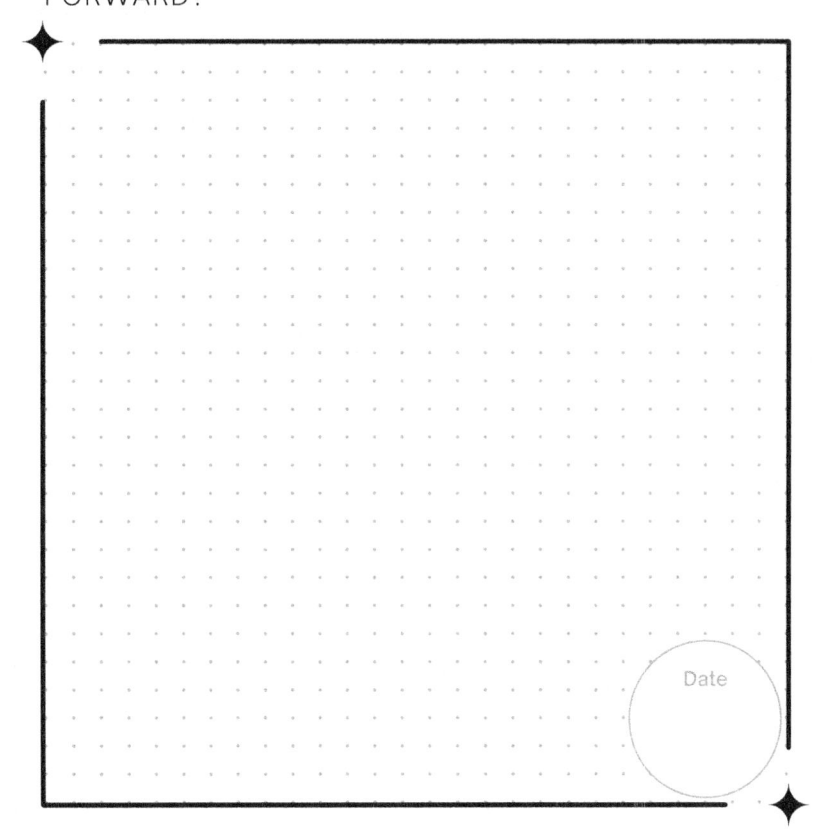

Date

Chapter 4

THE BEST AND FASTEST WAY TO CHANGE SOMEONE

- **Acceptance Over Resistance:** Accepting your partner's hobbies or habits, even if you don't personally enjoy them, can improve your relationship instantly.
- **Reflect on Your Own Habits:** Recognize that you might have habits that others find annoying too, and understand that changing oneself is hard, so it's unfair to try to change others.
- **Build Intimacy Through Acceptance:** By simply saying "okay" and allowing your partner to enjoy their interests without judgment, you can foster a more loving and intimate relationship.

HOW CAN I PRACTICE MORE ACCEPTANCE IN MY RELATIONSHIPS, AND WHAT HABIT OR INTEREST OF MY PARTNER OR FRIENDS CAN I START ACCEPTING TODAY?

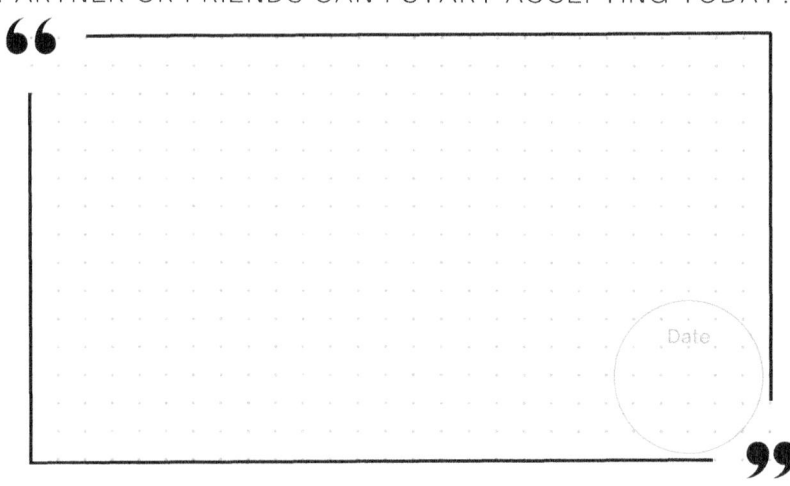

Date

Chapter 5

YOU ARE BIGGER THAN WHAT'S MAKING YOU ANXIOUS

- **Perspective Shift:** Moving or changing your environment can provide a fresh perspective, revealing that your current worries are smaller in the grand scheme of things.
- **Multiple Communities:** Your current community is just one of many you can belong to, and if one fails you, there are countless others you can join.
- **Endless Possibilities:** You have the power to start over and create new opportunities for yourself, no matter how difficult or scary it might seem.

HOW CAN I REMIND MYSELF OF THE ENDLESS POSSIBILITIES AVAILABLE TO ME, AND TAKE A SMALL STEP TODAY TO EXPLORE A NEW OPPORTUNITY?

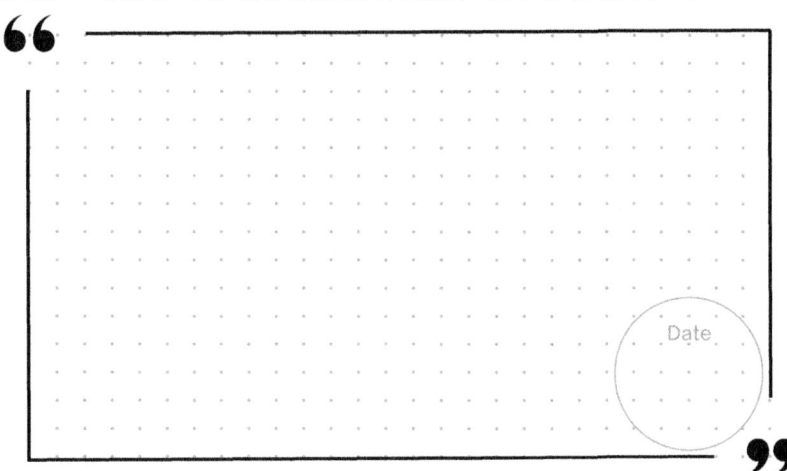

Date

Chapter 6

LIVING YOUR DREAMS CAN START RIGHT THIS SECOND

- **Start Now:** Living your dreams doesn't require perfect timing or grand gestures. Small, consistent actions can align your daily life with your bigger aspirations.
- **Reflect Honestly:** Compare your dreams with your current daily activities. Identify where you are out of sync and make adjustments.
- **Simple Steps Matter:** Even small actions like setting aside time or money can significantly impact achieving your dreams.

MY KEY TAKE AWAY

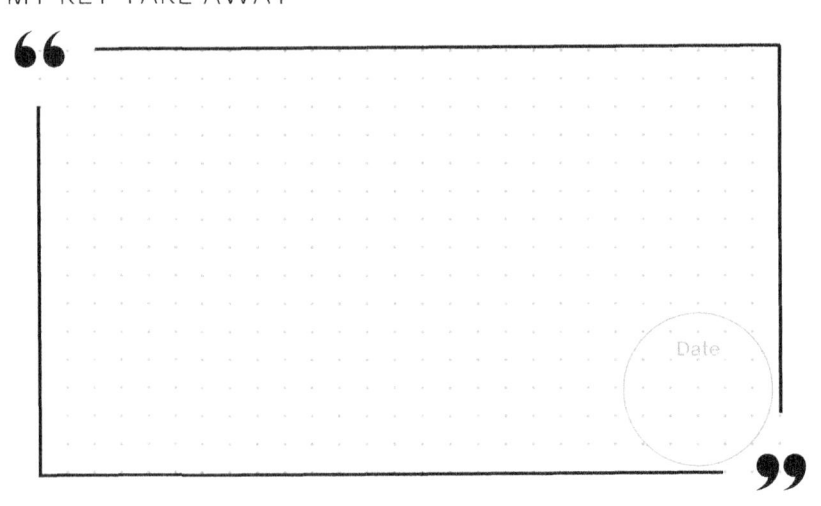

Date

Journal

FIVE BIG DREAMS I HAVE FOR MY LIFE

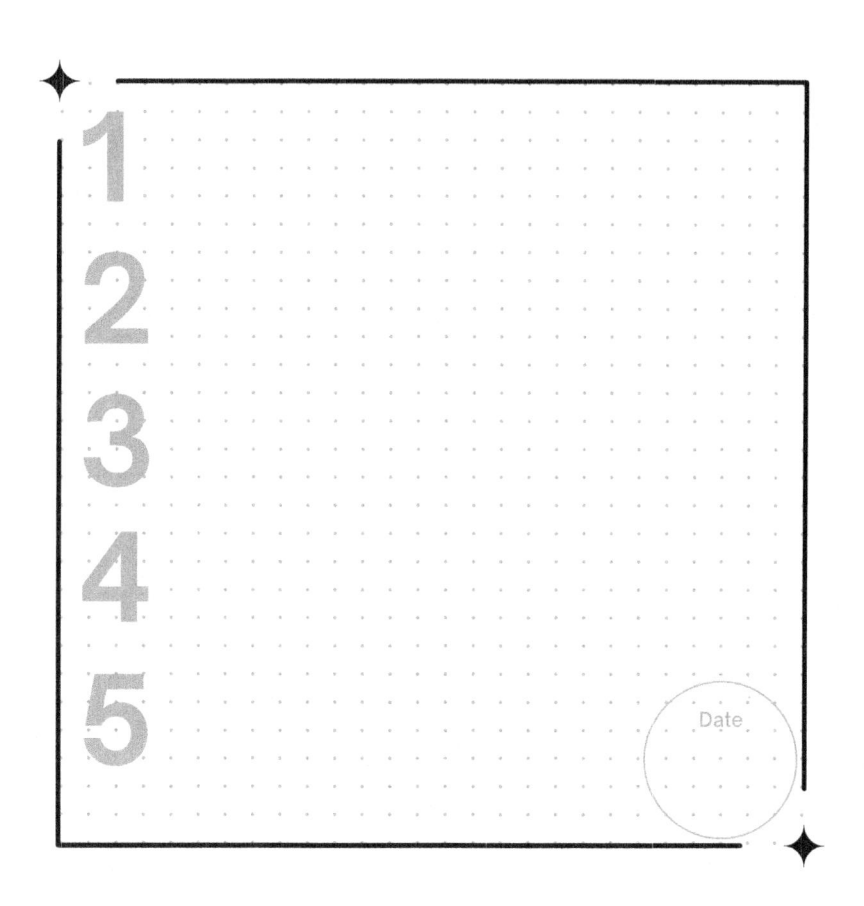

1
2
3
4
5

Date

Journal

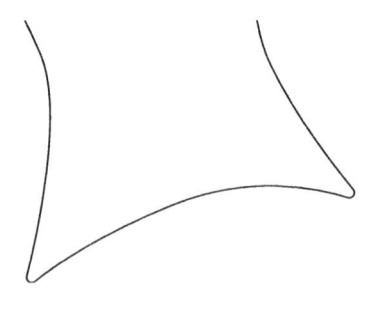

THE TRUTH ABOUT WHAT MY FIVE LAST DAYS
REALLY LOOKED LIKE

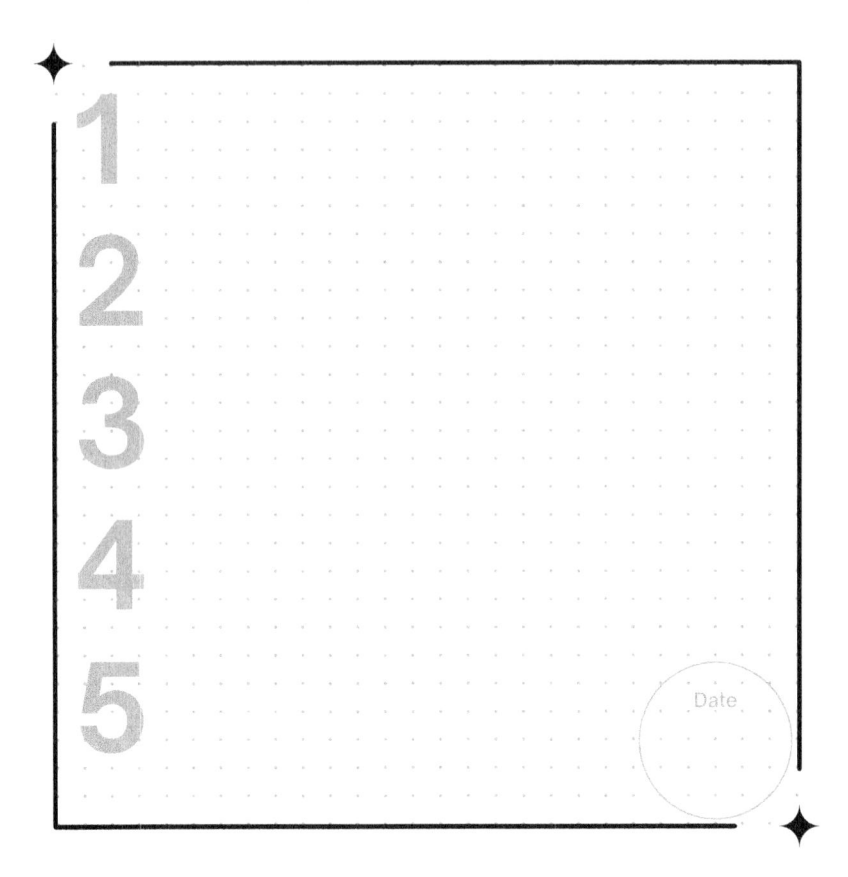

1

2

3

4

5

Date

Journal

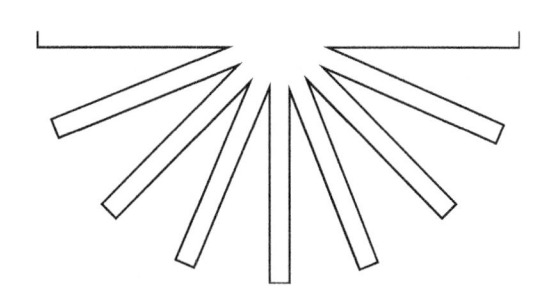

FIVE EASY THINGS I CAN DO OR PLAN RIGHT NOW TO SUPPORT MY FIVE BIG DREAMS

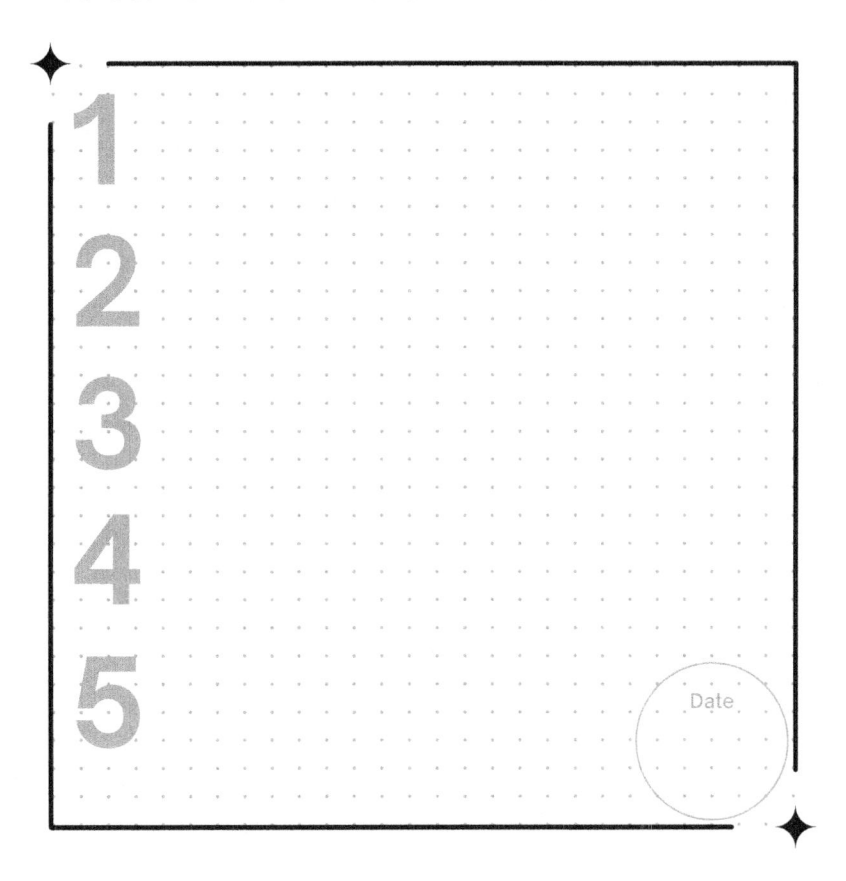

1.
2.
3.
4.
5.

Date

Chapter 7

IF SOMETHING FEELS OFF, IT PROBABLY IS

- **Trust Your Intuition:** If something feels off, it likely is. Listen to your gut feelings in relationships, investments, and other areas of life.
- **Seek Clarity:** Everything in life should be easy to understand. If you can't explain it simply, it may be a red flag.
- **Avoid Complication:** Life shouldn't be complicated. Steer clear of gray areas and situations that feel confusing or uneasy.

HOW CAN I BETTER LISTEN TO MY GUT FEELINGS MOVING FORWARD?

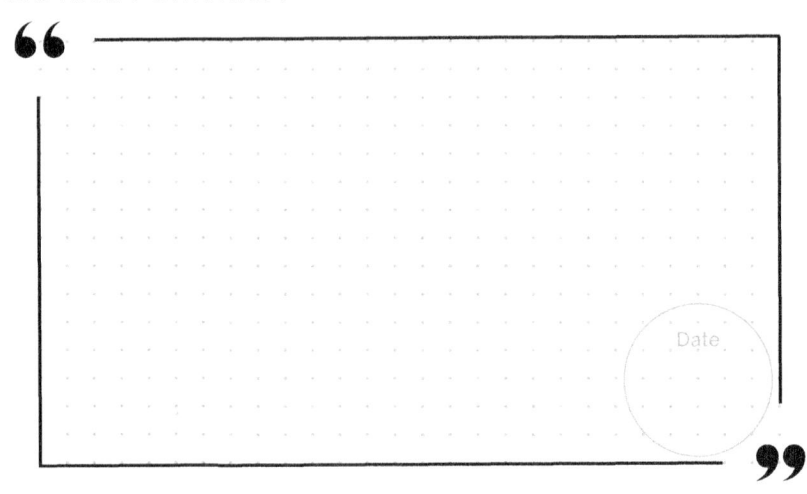

"

Date

"

Chapter 8

IT'S OKAY TO BE SAD AFTER MAKING THE RIGHT DECISION

- **Sadness Is Normal:** It's natural to feel sad even after making the right decision. Emotions are part of the healing process.
- **Accept Your Emotions:** Allow yourself to fully experience sadness. It's a valid and essential part of being human.
- **Right Choices Can Be Difficult:** Doing what's right isn't always easy. Sadness doesn't mean the decision was wrong; it means you're human.

HOW CAN I BETTER EMBRACE AND ACCEPT MY FEELINGS OF SADNESS AFTER MAKING A TOUGH DECISION?

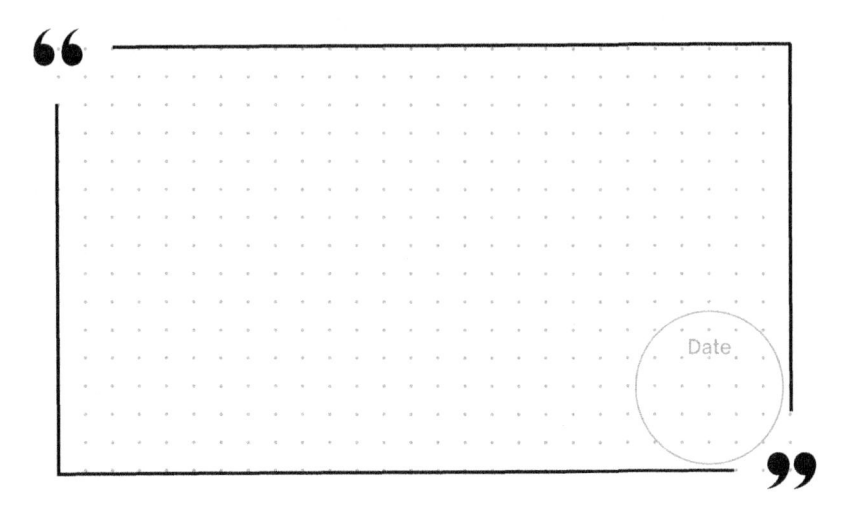

"

Date

"

Chapter 9

WHAT TO REMEMBER WHEN YOU MESS UP

- **Self-Compassion in Mistakes:** When you make a mistake, remind yourself that not knowing is normal and forgive yourself.
- **Learning Process:** Life is about learning and improving. When you learn better, you do better.
- **Grace Towards Others:** Extend the same understanding to others when they make mistakes.

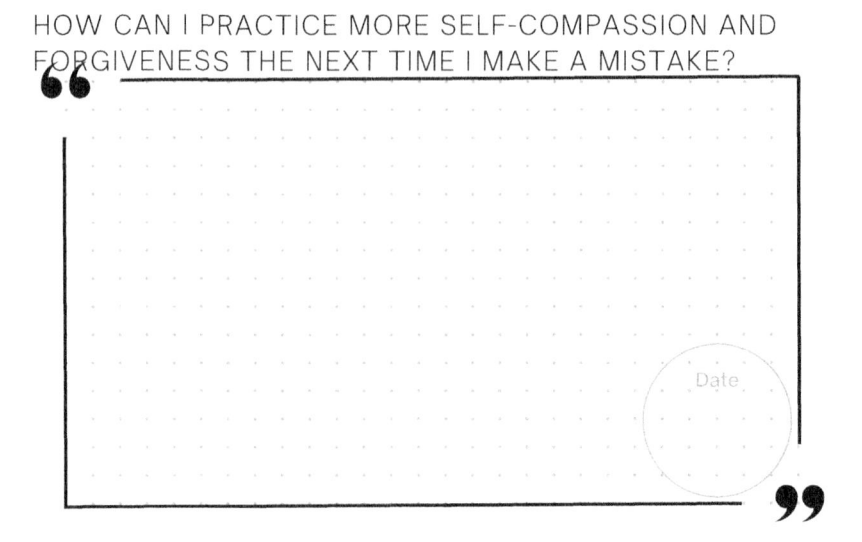

HOW CAN I PRACTICE MORE SELF-COMPASSION AND FORGIVENESS THE NEXT TIME I MAKE A MISTAKE?

Date

Chapter 10

CALL YOUR TO-DO-LIST YOUR "GET-TO-DO-LIST"

- **Shift Your Perspective:** Transform your to-do list into a "get-to-do" list to foster gratitude and appreciation for daily tasks.
- **Gratitude for Opportunities:** Recognize the privileges and opportunities behind each task, such as access to healthcare or the trust of clients.
- **Positive Mindset:** A positive outlook can change how you feel about your responsibilities, making them feel less like chores and more like opportunities.

WHICH OF MY DAILY TASKS DO I WISH TO REFRAME INTO OPPORTUNITIES RATHER THAN OBLIGATIONS?

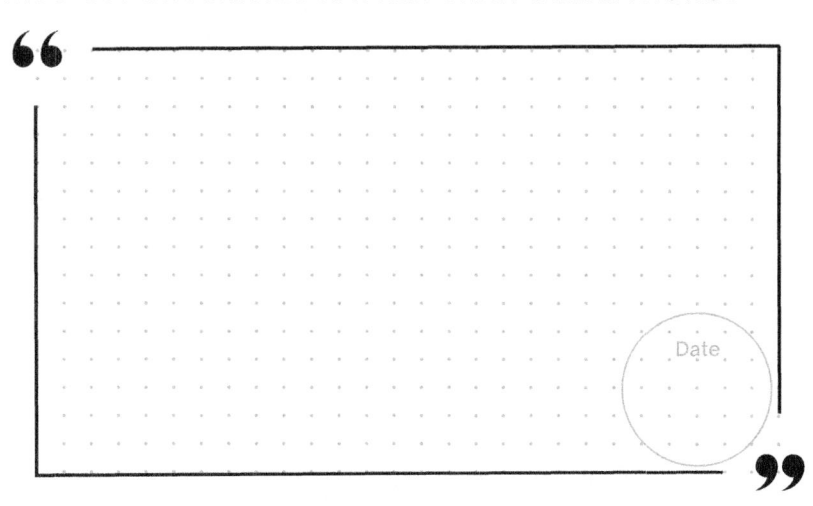

Date

Chapter 11

ORDINARY ROUTINES CREATE EXTRAORDINARY RESULTS

- **Daily Actions Matter:** Consistent, repetitive actions are essential for achieving your vision. Each small task contributes to a larger goal.
- **Take Breaks:** Humans need breaks to maintain enthusiasm and productivity. It's okay to step back and recharge.
- **Remember the Vision:** Keeping the bigger picture in mind can help you stay motivated through mundane routines. Regularly remind yourself why you started and where you want to go.

HOW CAN I REMIND MYSELF OF MY BIGGER VISION EACH DAY TO STAY MOTIVATED THROUGH MY DAILY ROUTINES?

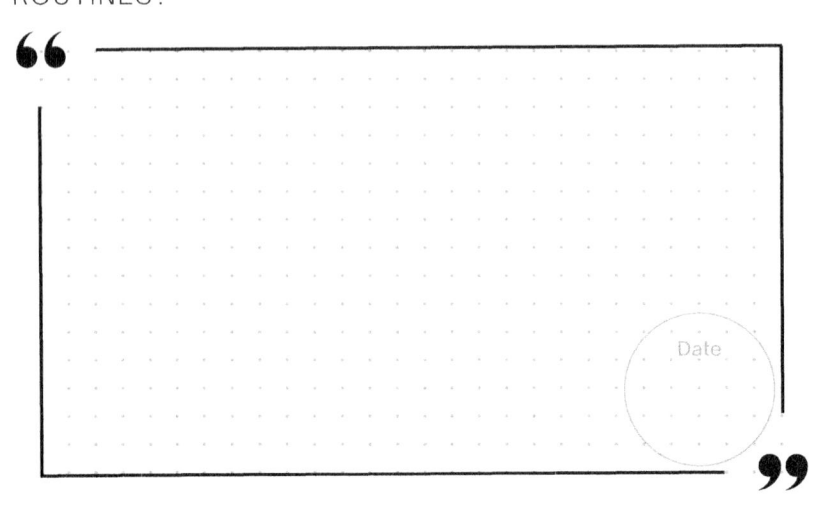

Date

Chapter 12

WEAR OUT, DON'T RUST OUT, BABY

- **Live Boldly:** Life is meant for adventure and contribution, not just safety and comfort.
- **Embrace Wear and Tear:** Engage fully with life, accepting the wear and tear that comes from living passionately.
- **Temporary and Unique:** Recognize and embrace your unique, temporary existence, making the most of your time.

HOW CAN I FULLY EMBRACE LIFE TODAY, TAKING RISKS AND LIVING BOLDLY RATHER THAN STAYING IN MY COMFORT ZONE?

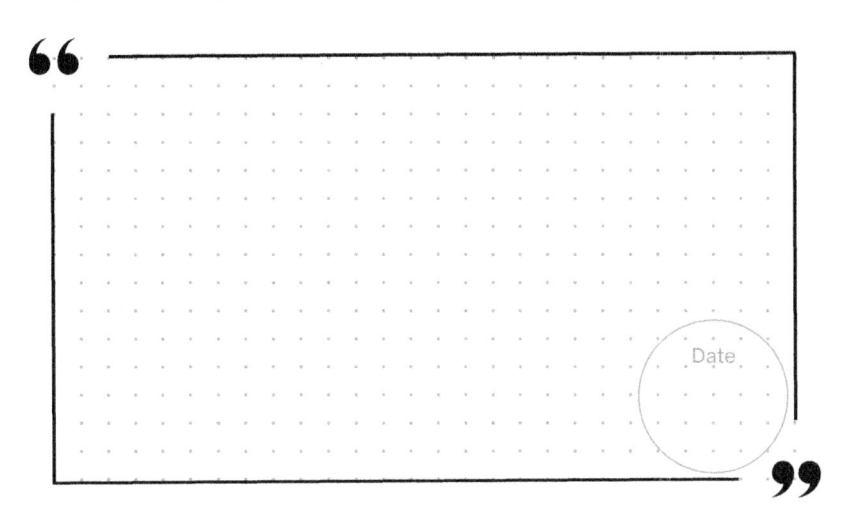

> Date

Chapter 13

COMMUNICATE WITHOUT CONFUSION

- **Set Clear Expectations:** Avoid misunderstandings by clearly communicating your plans and preferences.
- **Ask Questions:** Clarify others' expectations to prevent assumptions and miscommunications.
- **Respectful Communication:** Clear communication shows respect and helps maintain positive relationships.

WHAT IS ONE AREA WHERE I FEEL MISUNDERSTOOD AND NEED TO IMPROVE MY COMMUNICATION?

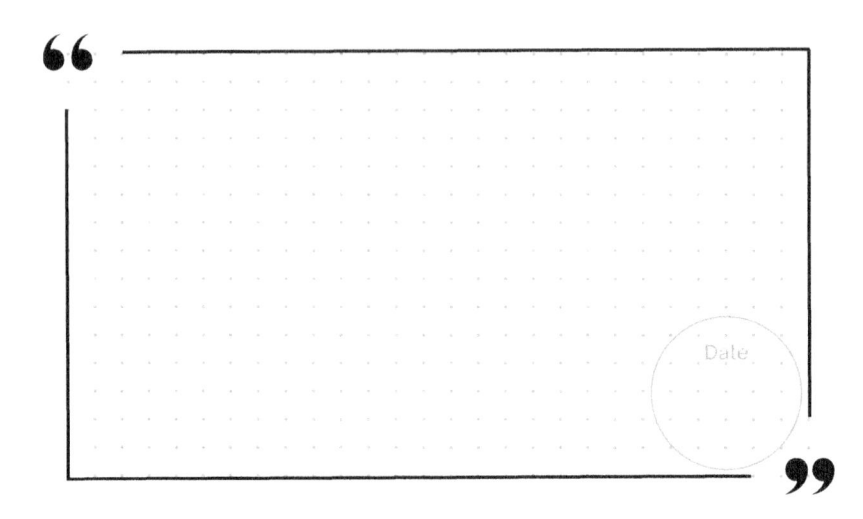

"

Date

"

Chapter 14

YOU DON'T HAVE TO DEFEND YOURSELF, EVER

- **Embrace Vulnerability:** Show your true self, including flaws. It can be empowering and disarm critics.
- **Let Go of Defensiveness:** Defensiveness is ego-driven and distorts situations. Being authentic without defense can lead to freedom and success.
- **Self-Acceptance:** Accept and acknowledge your flaws openly. It saves energy and builds genuine connections.

WHAT PARTS OF MYSELF DO I DEFEND OR HIDE? HOW CAN I CHANGE MY LIFE IF I EMBRACED THESE PARTS FULLY?

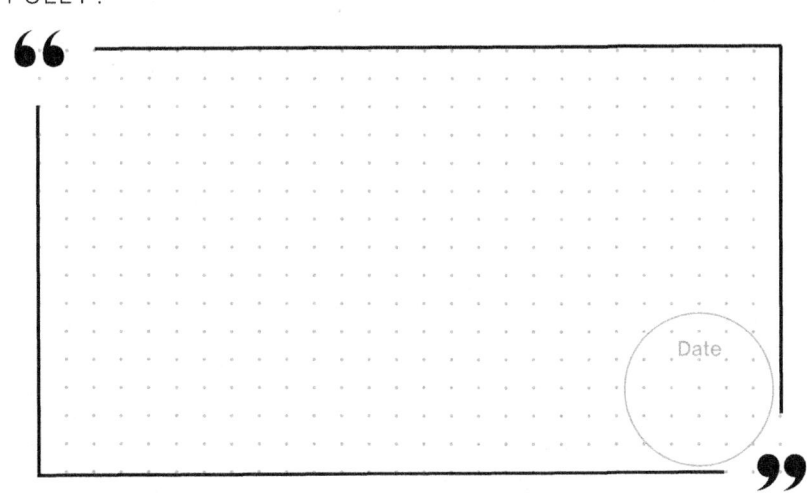

"

Date

"

Chapter 15

SUCCESS IS VERY UNSEXY

- **Embrace Repetition:** Success often involves mastering basic tasks through repetitive practice. Consistent effort, even if mundane, leads to mastery.
- **Focus on Consistency:** Success isn't about quick wins or lucky breaks. It's about showing up regularly and doing the necessary work over time.
- **Acknowledge Behind-the-Scenes Work:** The visible success is often built on unseen, tedious effort. Recognize and appreciate the repetitive tasks that contribute to success.

WHAT BORING OR REPETITIVE TASKS AM I CURRENTLY AVOIDING, EVEN THOUGH THEY CAN HELP ME ACHIEVE MY GOALS?

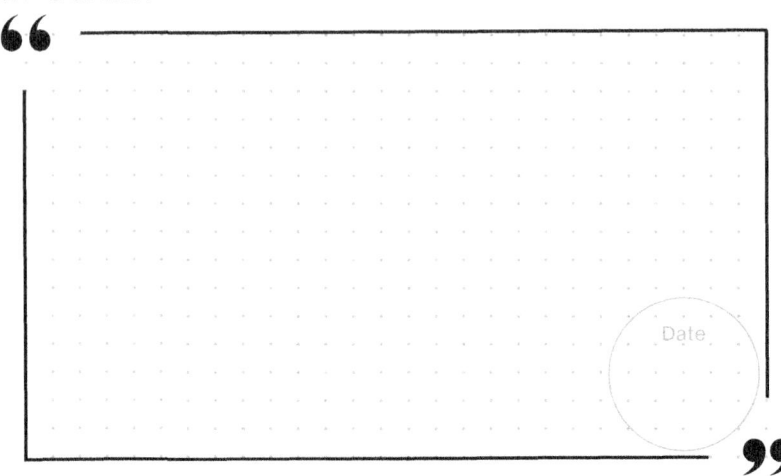

Date

Chapter 16

DRIFTING OFF YOUR LIFE'S COURSE HAPPENS SLOWLY

- **Awareness of Drifting:** Just like drifting in the ocean, you may drift away from your life goals without realizing it. Stay aware of your direction.
- **Set Clear Goals:** To prevent drifting, establish clear goals and regularly measure your progress against them.
- **Focus and Intention:** Focused intention can guide you back on track more effectively than reacting to invisible changes.

WHAT AREAS OF MY LIFE HAVE I BEEN DRIFTING IN, AND HOW CAN I SET CLEAR GOALS TO REDIRECT MYSELF?

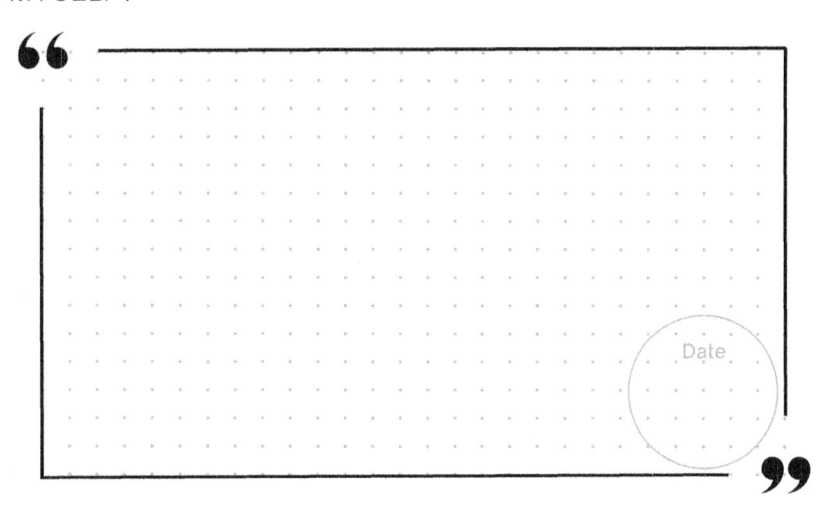

Date

Chapter 17

BEST THING I NEVER HAD IS THE BEST BEYONCE SONG

- **Embrace Unwanted Outcomes:** Sometimes, not getting what you thought you wanted turns out to be a blessing in disguise.
- **Align with Your True Desires:** It's crucial to recognize and pursue what genuinely makes you happy, rather than what others expect or value.
- **Recognize the Benefits of Letting Go:** Letting go of things that don't serve you—whether it's a relationship, job, or belief—can open doors to better opportunities and happiness.

WHAT IS SOMETHING I INITIALLY WANTED BUT AM NOW THANKFUL DIDN'T WORK OUT?

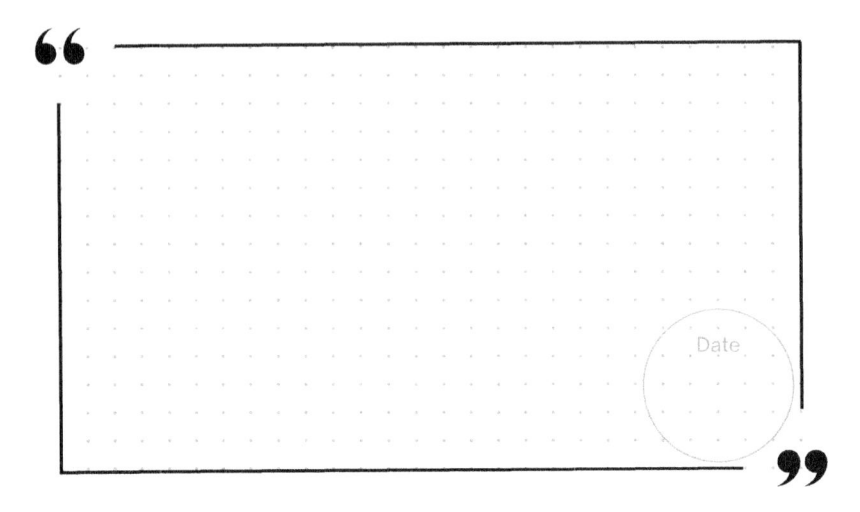

Date

Chapter 18

TAKE YOURSELF OUT TO LUNCH

- **Value Solitude:** Spending quality time alone can help you reconnect with your personal goals and enjoy your own company.
- **Self-Recognition:** Acknowledge and celebrate your achievements, whether big or small, to boost your self-esteem.
- **Moment Appreciation:** Every moment, including now, is vital and worthy of enjoyment. Embrace the present fully.

HOW CAN I INCORPORATE MORE SOLO ACTIVITIES INTO MY ROUTINE TO ENHANCE MY SELF-AWARENESS AND APPRECIATION?

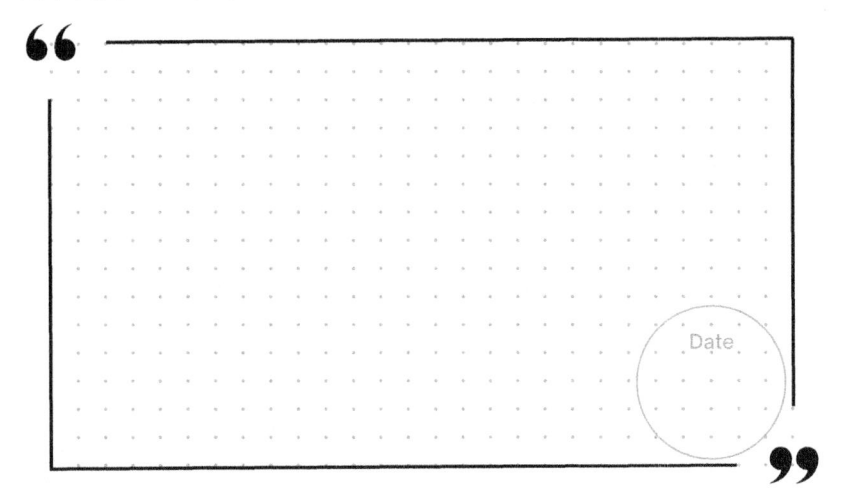

Date

Chapter 19

WHAT TO KNOW WHEN YOU'RE NOT SOMEONE'S CUP OF TEA

- **Accept Differences:** Understanding that not everyone will like or agree with you is key to personal peace.
- **Stay True to Yourself:** Maintain authenticity by being true to your values and beliefs despite external opinions.
- **Learn from Rejection:** Use rejection as an opportunity to strengthen your self-esteem and refine your social interactions.

HOW CAN I REMAIN MORE AUTHENTIC AND TRUE TO MYSELF WITHOUT WORRY FOR REJECTION OR DISAPPROVAL?

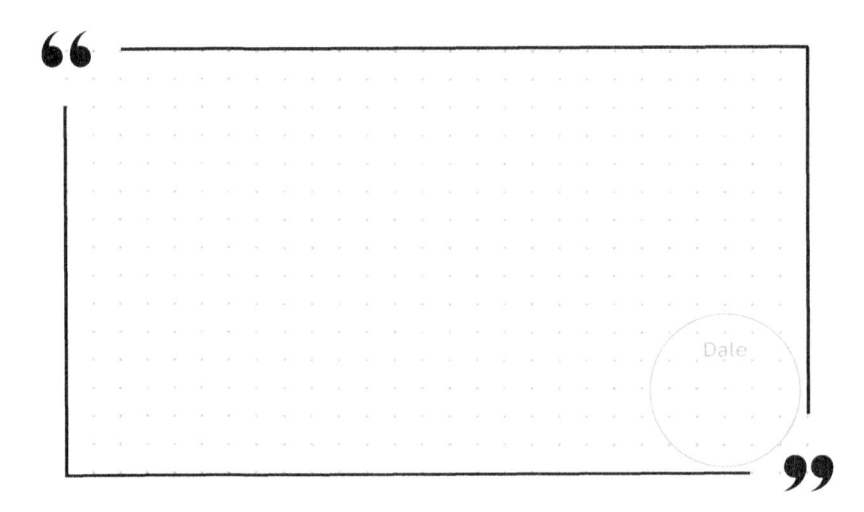

> Date

Chapter 20

STOP TRYING TO BALANCE EVERYTHING

- **Acknowledge Limits:** Recognize that seeking balance in every aspect of life can be unrealistic and stressful.
- **Prioritize Wisely:** Focus on what's most important at the moment and allow some flexibility in less critical areas.
- **Embrace Imbalance:** Sometimes, embracing the chaos can lead to greater personal growth and opportunities.

IN WHAT AREAS OF MY LIFE AM I FORCING BALANCE, AND HOW CAN I ADOPT A MORE FLEXIBLE APPROACH?

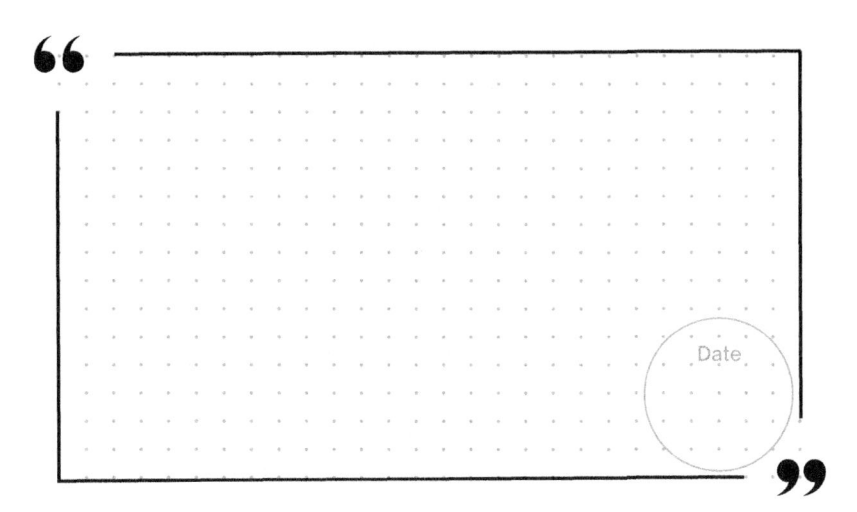

"

Date

"

Chapter 21

EVERYONE HAS INVISIBLE SCARS

- **Acknowledge Pain:** Recognize that everyone you meet may be dealing with hidden struggles or past trauma.
- **Offer Compassion:** Extend kindness and understanding to others, knowing that their actions may be influenced by unseen hardships.
- **Heal Through Sharing:** Sharing your experiences can help heal your scars and may encourage others to open up about their own.

WHAT INVISIBLE SCARS DO I CARRY, AND HOW HAVE THEY MADE ME STRONGER AND SMARTER?

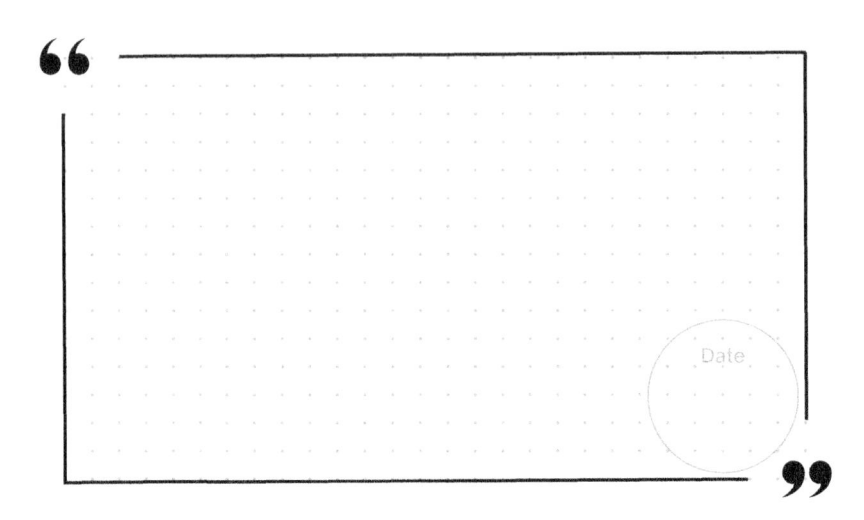

"

Date

"

Chapter 22

SEE THE WORLD IN HIGH DEFINITION

- **Engage Fully:** Experience life directly rather than through digital screens. Make real-world interactions a priority.
- **Reduce Digital Distraction:** Limit social media and digital distractions to enhance your real-life experiences.
- **Appreciate the Moment:** Focus on the richness of the world around you, appreciating the beauty in everyday moments.

WHICH IMPORTANT EXPERIENCES HAVE I HAD THAT WERE NOT EASY TO SHARE BUT DEEPLY MATTERED TO ME?

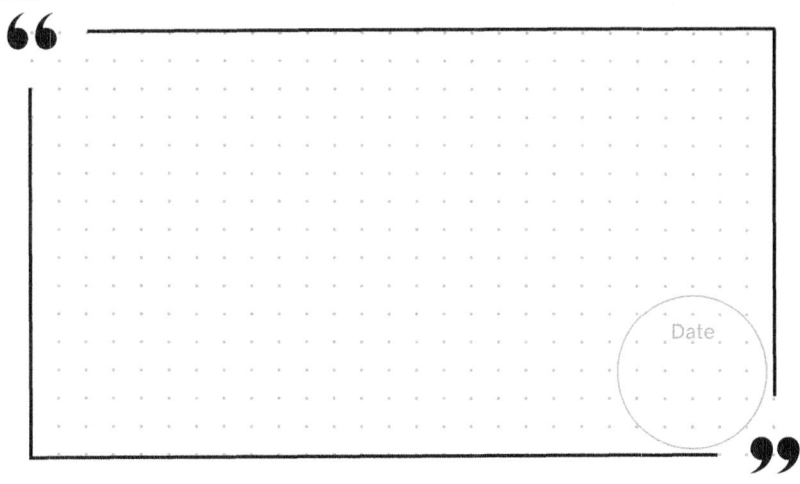

Date

Chapter 23

A LITTLE EXTRA MAKES ALL THE DIFFERENCE

- **Small Efforts Matter:** Even minor additional efforts in your daily tasks can lead to significant positive changes.
- **Consistency Pays Off:** Regular small improvements accumulate over time, enhancing your skills and relationships.
- **Rewarding Persistence:** Staying persistent in your efforts, no matter how small, can yield unexpected rewards and satisfaction.

WHERE CAN I PUT IN A LITTLE EXTRA EFFORT IN MY DAILY ACTIVITIES TO SEE SUBSTANTIAL LONG-TERM BENEFITS?

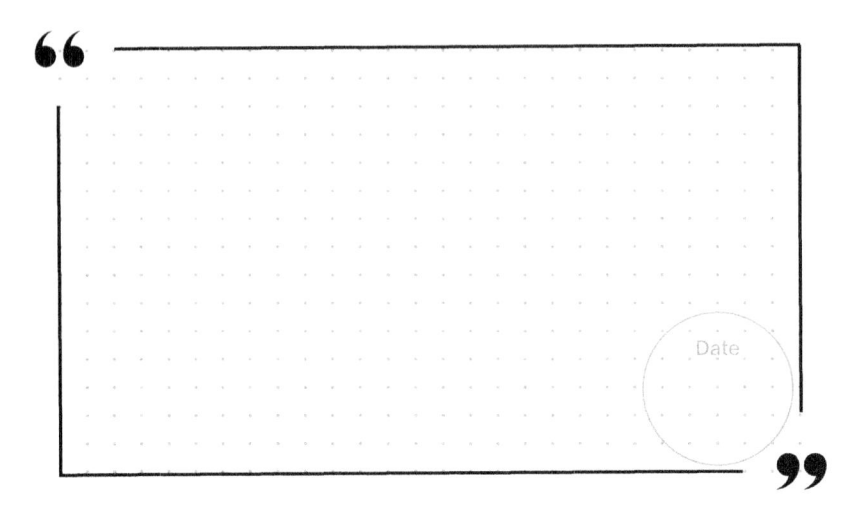

"

Date

"

Chapter 24

BE EASY ABOUT SEX

- **Open Communication:** Foster an environment where sexual needs and desires can be openly discussed without judgment.
- **Emotional Connection:** Strengthen your emotional connection to enhance physical intimacy.
- **Respect Boundaries:** Always respect personal and emotional boundaries to maintain a healthy and satisfying sexual relationship.

WHERE CAN I CHOOSE TO MAKE MY PARTNER RIGHT INSTEAD OF WRONG, AND BE CURIOUS INSTEAD OF JUDGMENTAL?

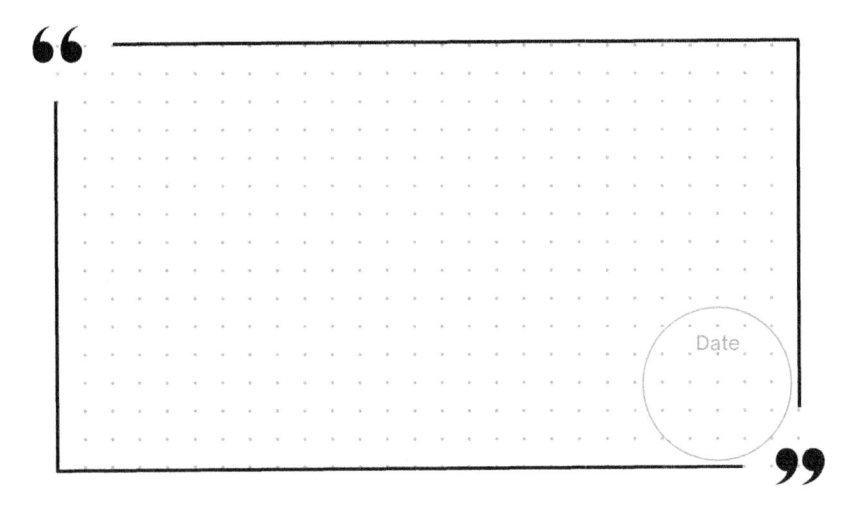

"

Date

"

Chapter 25

ARGUE FOR YOUR POSSIBILITIES

- **Challenge Self-Doubt:** Actively argue against your own self-imposed limitations and embrace your potential.
- **Advocate for Yourself:** Be your own biggest supporter in personal and professional settings.
- **Expand Your Beliefs:** Regularly update your beliefs about what you are capable of achieving.

HOW CAN I BETTER ADVOCATE FOR MY POSSIBILITIES AND CHALLENGE MY SELF-IMPOSED LIMITS?

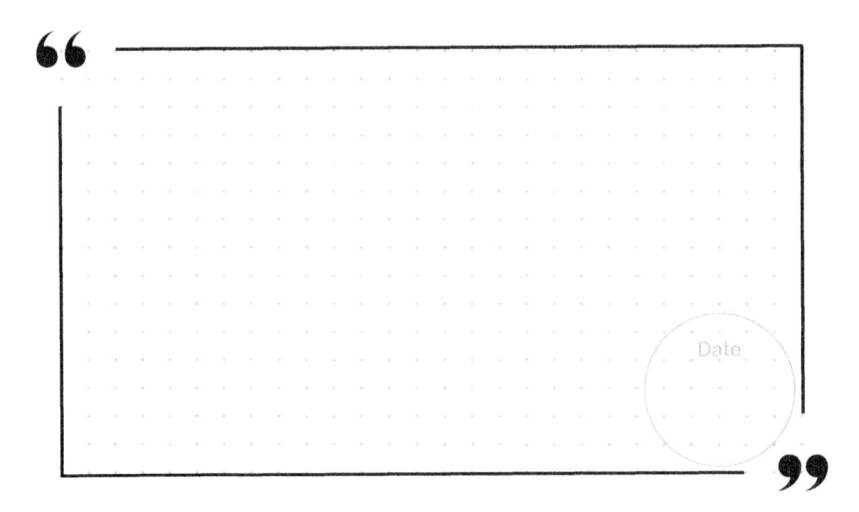

"

Date

"

Chapter 26

JUST DECIDE

- **Trust Your Instincts:** Confidence in decision-making comes from trusting your gut feelings.
- **Overcome Indecision:** Avoid paralysis by analysis by committing to decisions promptly.
- **Learn from Decisions:** Every decision, right or wrong, provides valuable lessons.

WHAT DECISION AM I DELAYING MAKING, AND WHAT IS MY QUICK DECISION?

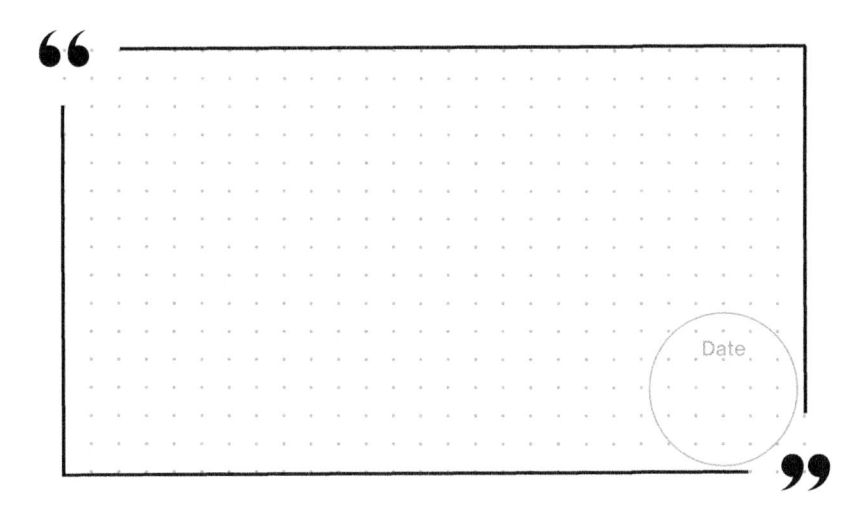

Date

Chapter 27

KNOW YOUR BLIND SPOTS

- **Identify Biases:** Acknowledge personal biases that may cloud judgment.
- **Seek Feedback:** Use external perspectives to reveal blind spots.
- **Continuous Improvement:** Regularly reevaluate beliefs and knowledge to address overlooked areas.

WHAT AM I MISSING OUT ON, AND HOW CAN I ACTIVELY WORK TO UNCOVER MY BLIND SPOTS TO LIVE A BIGGER LIFE?

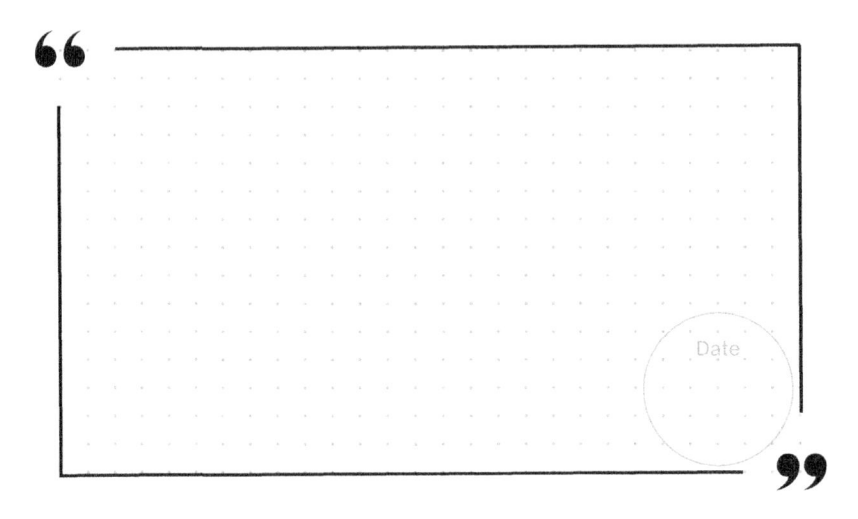

Date.

Chapter 28

CONFIDENCE IS SIMPLY A WILLINGNESS TO FEEL UNCOMFORTABLE

- **Embrace Discomfort:** True confidence comes from facing and growing through discomfort.
- **Pursue Challenges:** Confidence builds when you regularly step out of your comfort zone.
- **Resilience Development:** Learning to deal with uncomfortable feelings leads to stronger resilience.

IN WHAT AREAS OF MY LIFE DO I AVOID DISCOMFORT, AND HOW CAN I BEGIN TO EMBRACE CHALLENGES TO BUILD CONFIDENCE?

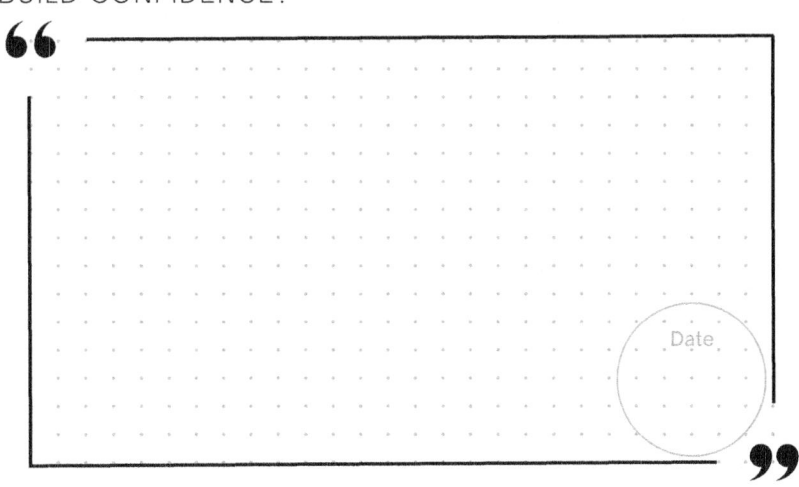

Date

Chapter 29

THE PAST DOES NOT CREATE THE PRESENT

- **Break from the Past:** Understand that past conditions do not dictate current or future possibilities.
- **Create New Paths:** Actively choose actions that diverge from past patterns.
- **Empowerment through Choice:** Embrace the power to redefine your life, regardless of your history.

HOW DOES MY PAST INFLUENCE MY PRESENT, AND WHAT STEPS CAN I TAKE TO CREATE A FUTURE THAT IS NOT BOUND BY IT?

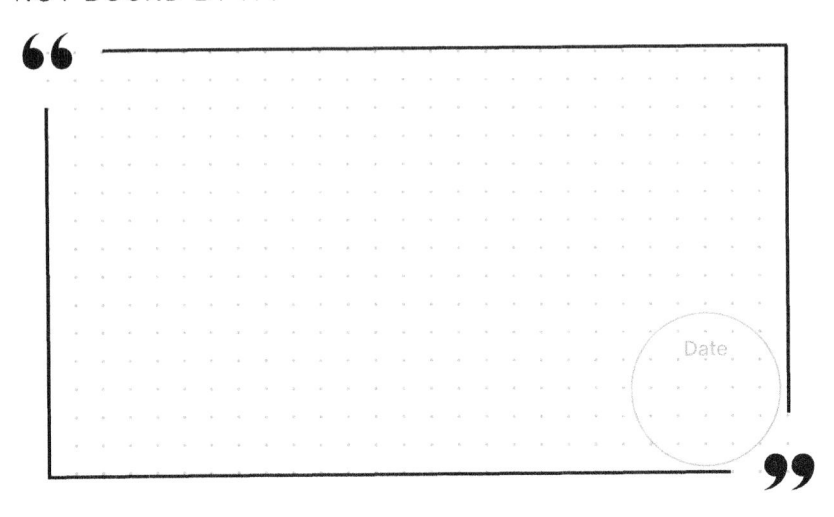

Date

Chapter 30

DESIRE IS THE GREATEST FORCE IN HUMAN NATURE

- **Harness Desire:** Channel deep desires into constructive action.
- **Align Goals with Desires:** Ensure your goals are deeply connected to your intrinsic motivations.
- **Sustain Momentum:** Use the energy from desires to maintain persistence towards goals.

WHAT ARE MY DEEPEST DESIRE, AND HOW WILL I WORK FOR IT?

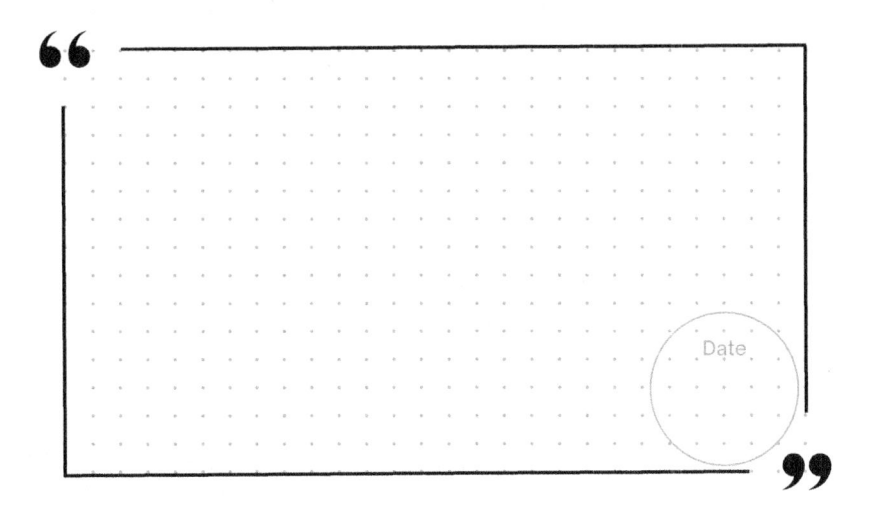

"

Date

"

Chapter 31

GRIEF IS LOVE

- **Embrace Grief as an Expression of Love:** Recognize that deep grief is a testament to deep love.
- **Healing through Acceptance:** Accept grief as a natural, necessary process.
- **Honor Loved Ones:** Use memories and legacy as a way to transform grief into a loving tribute.

HOW CAN I VIEW MY EXPERIENCES OF GRIEF AS A REFLECTION OF MY CAPACITY FOR LOVE, AND HOW CAN THIS PERSPECTIVE HELP ME HEAL?

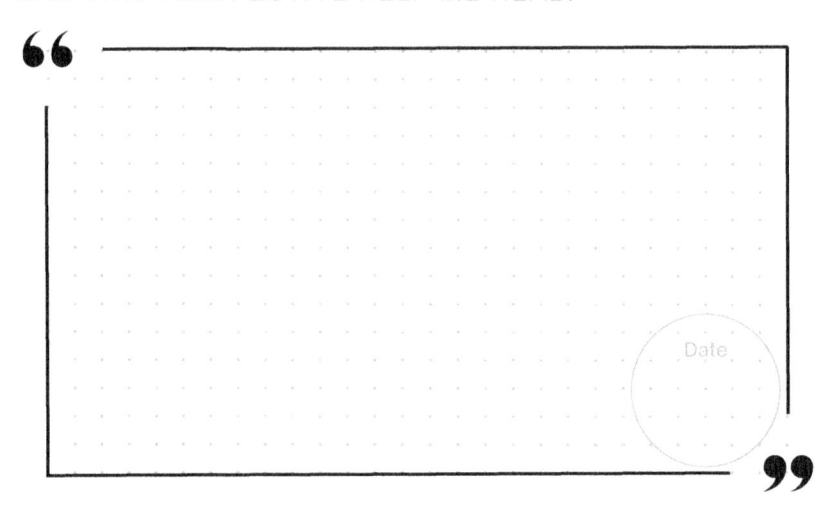

Date

Chapter 32

EVERY SILVER LINING HAS A CLOUD, AND THAT'S OKAY

- **Accept Contrasts:** Embrace the natural duality of joy and sorrow in life.
- **Find Balance:** Understand that feeling sad about good things ending is part of valuing them.
- **Resilience in Duality:** Build emotional resilience by accepting and preparing for life's ups and downs.

IN WHAT WAYS DOES MY SADNESS REVEAL WHAT I TRULY CARE ABOUT?

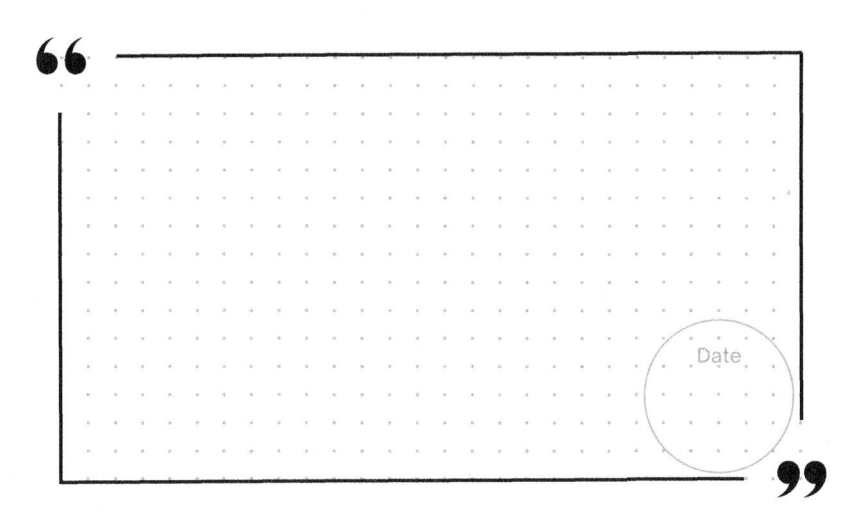

Date

Chapter 33

LET PEOPLE KNOW YOU'RE HAPPY TO SEE THEM

- **Show Enthusiasm:** Demonstrate genuine happiness when meeting people.
- **Build Connections:** Use warmth and interest to foster deeper relationships.
- **Positive Interactions:** Create a welcoming atmosphere that encourages positive exchanges.

WHO DO I WANT TO GET BETTER AT SHOWING MY APPRECIATION TO, AND HOW?

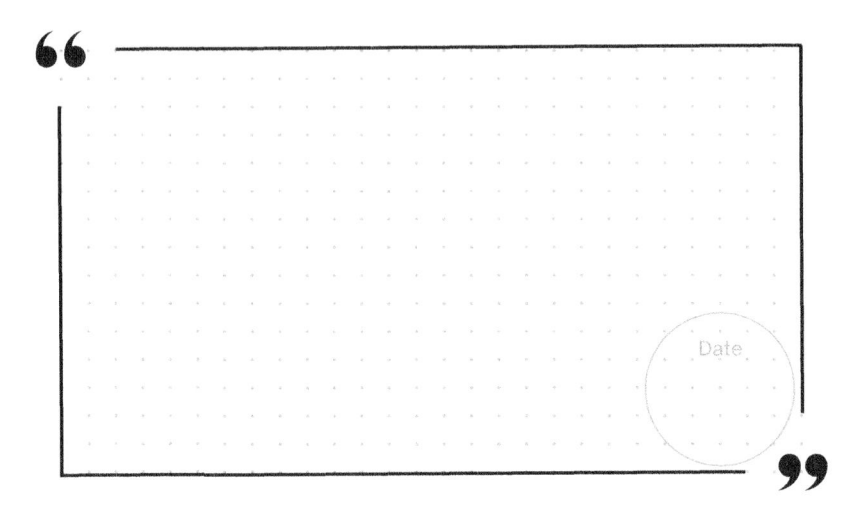

Date

Chapter 34

THE NEXT TIME SOMEONE GIVES YOU A WEIRD LOOK

- **Don't Assume:** Avoid jumping to conclusions based on others' expressions or reactions.
- **Seek Clarity:** If unsure, ask directly about the other person's thoughts or feelings.
- **Maintain Self-Confidence:** Trust in your value and don't let misunderstandings shake your confidence.

ARE THERE SITUATIONS WHERE I'VE BLAMED MYSELF WITHOUT REALLY KNOWING IF IT WAS MY FAULT?

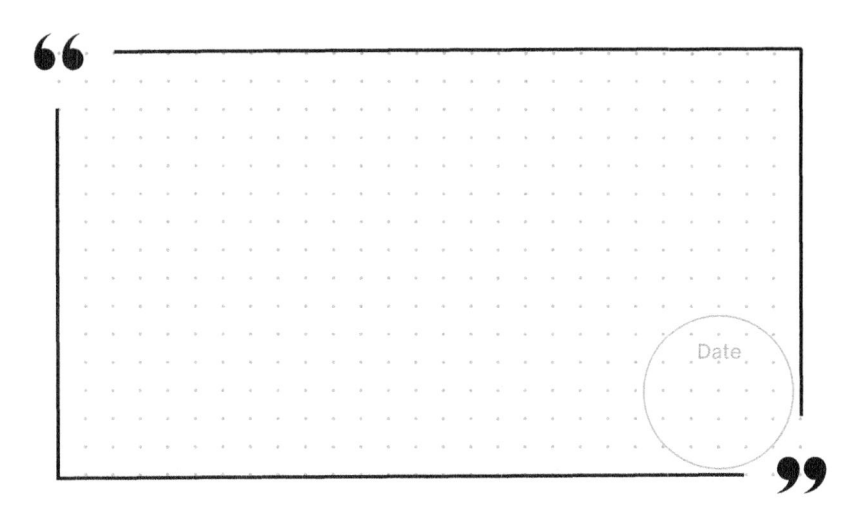

"

Date

"

Chapter 35

GOOD AND BAD, YOU'LL GET USED TO IT

- **Adaptability**: Humans quickly adapt to both positive and negative changes.
- **Manage Expectations**: Adjust expectations to maintain satisfaction with life's ebbs and flows.
- **Savor Moments**: Take time to appreciate positive changes before they become the norm.

WHAT AM I GRATEFUL FOR? AND WHAT DO I HAVE NOW THAT I DIDN'T HAVE A YEAR AGO?

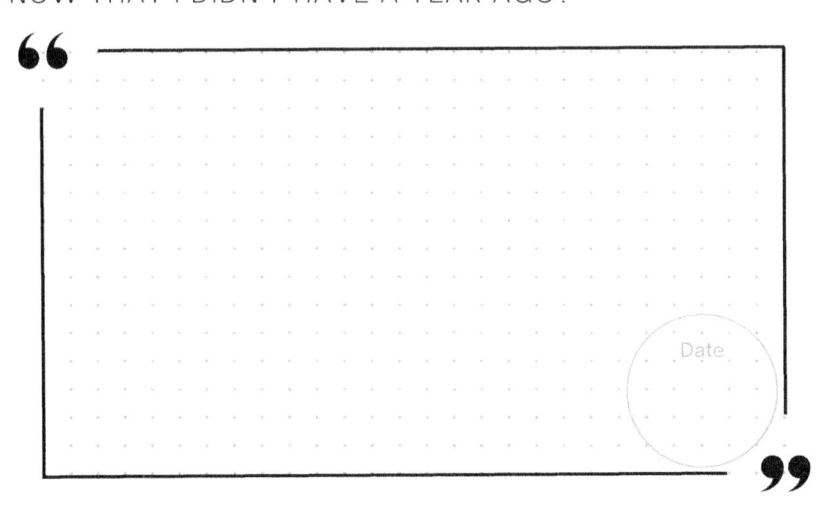

> Date

Chapter 36

IF YOU DON'T FEEL LIKE AN IMPOSTER, ARE YOU REALLY GOING FOR IT?

- **Normalize Imposter Syndrome:** Understand that feeling like an imposter can signify growth and high standards.
- **Challenge Yourself:** Use imposter feelings as motivation to continue pushing your boundaries.
- **Seek Support:** Discuss your feelings with mentors or peers who can provide perspective and support.

IN WHAT SITUATIONS DO I FEEL LIKE AN IMPOSTER, AND HOW CAN I USE THESE FEELINGS TO FUEL MY PERSONAL GROWTH?

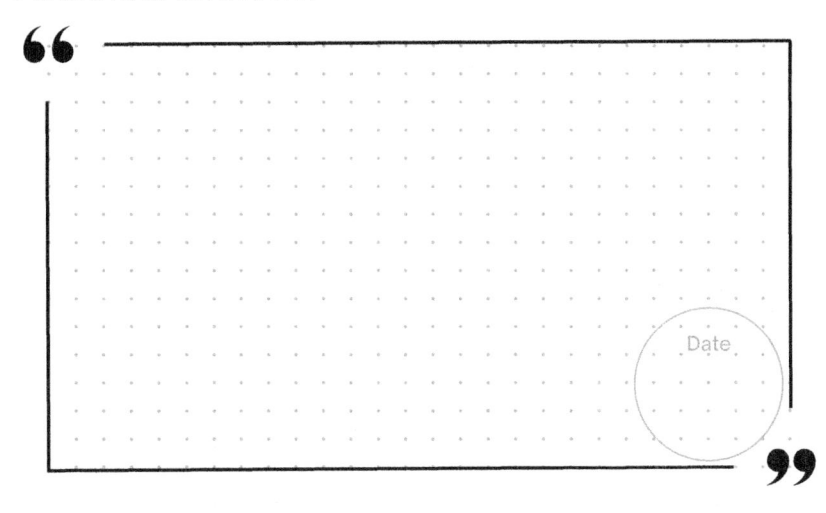

Date

Chapter 37

IF THEY GOSSIP TO YOU, THEY'LL GOSSIP ABOUT YOU

- **Awareness of Gossip:** Recognize that those who gossip to you likely gossip about you as well.
- **Maintain Integrity:** Choose not to participate in gossip to uphold your personal integrity.
- **Build Trustworthy Relationships:** Foster relationships with those who communicate openly and respectfully.

WHEN DO I GOSSIP? AND WHO AM I GOSSIPING WITH AND CAN I STOP IT OR AVOID IT?

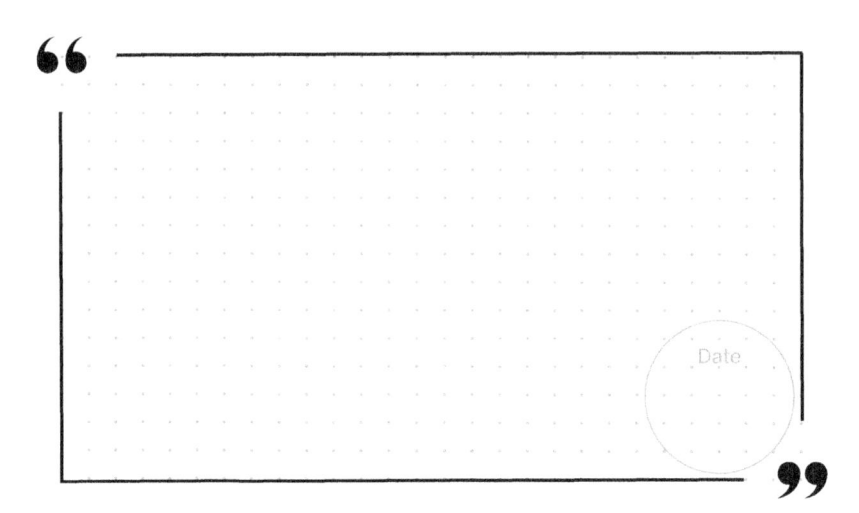

Chapter 38

CALL ON YOUR IMAGINARY MENTORS

- **Use Role Models:** Draw on the wisdom of role models, even if they are not physically present.
- **Guidance in Decision-Making:** Let the principles of your mentors guide your decisions and actions.
- **Inspiration for Challenges:** Use the success and integrity of your mentors as inspiration during challenging times.

WHO ARE MY IMAGINARY MENTORS, AND WHAT ADVICE WOULD THEY GIVE ME ABOUT THE CURRENT CHALLENGES I FACE?

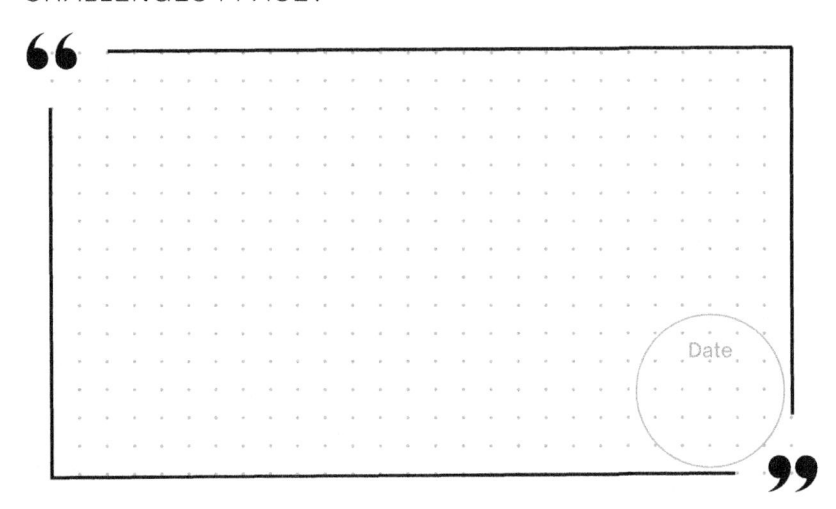

"

Date

"

Chapter 39

STOP SAYING I'M PROUD OF YOU

- **Encouragement Over Praise:** Shift from expressing pride to providing specific encouragement and recognition.
- **Foster Autonomy:** Help others feel self-motivated rather than seeking external validation.
- **Deepen Connections:** Use personalized encouragement to deepen connections and understanding.

WHO CAN I PRAISE IN A MORE ENCOURAGING WAY AND HOW?

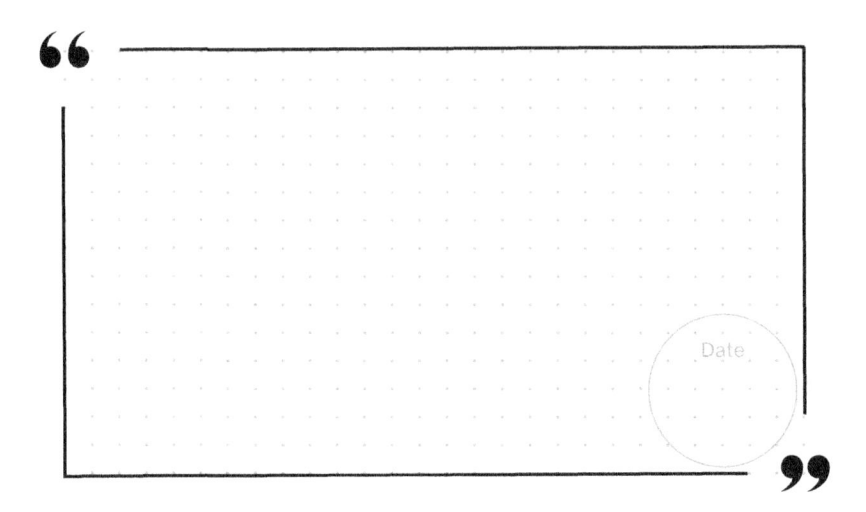

Chapter 40

THE BEST COACHING QUESTION EVER

- **Empower with Questions:** Use powerful questions to help others (and yourself) uncover hidden options and solutions.
- **Foster Self-Reflection:** Encourage a deeper exploration of personal desires, fears, and potential actions.
- **Cultivate Autonomy:** Help individuals realize they have the power to change their situations and outcomes.

WHAT DO I HAVE CONTROL OVER RIGHT NOW, AND HOW CAN I USE THAT TO POSITIVELY IMPACT MY CURRENT SITUATION?

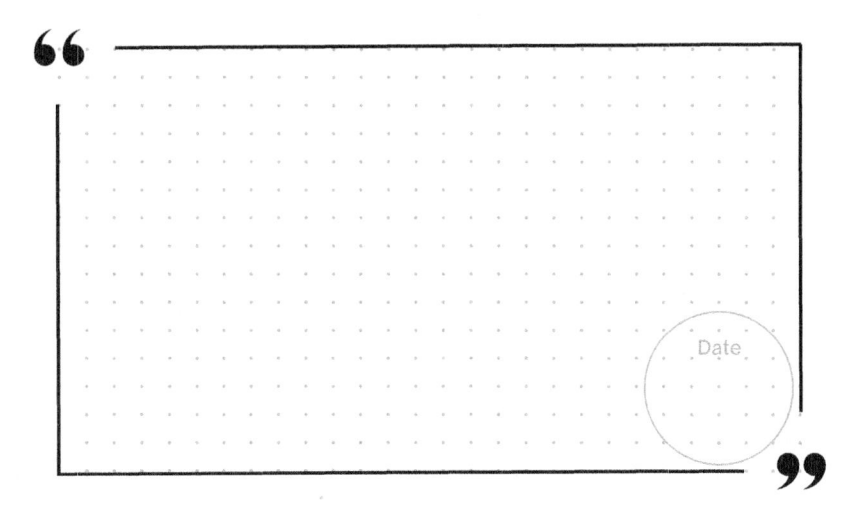

" "

Date

Chapter 41

THE GRASS IS GREENER BECAUSE IT'S FAKE

- **Challenge Perceptions:** Recognize that the seemingly perfect lives of others are often not as they appear.
- **Focus on Personal Growth:** Concentrate on your own achievements and growth rather than comparing to others.
- **Cultivate Authentic Satisfaction:** Find genuine contentment in your own life's journey, independent of external comparisons.

WHAT ASPECTS OF OTHERS' LIVES DO I OFTEN ENVY, AND HOW CAN I SHIFT MY FOCUS TO APPRECIATING AND IMPROVING MY OWN CIRCUMSTANCES?

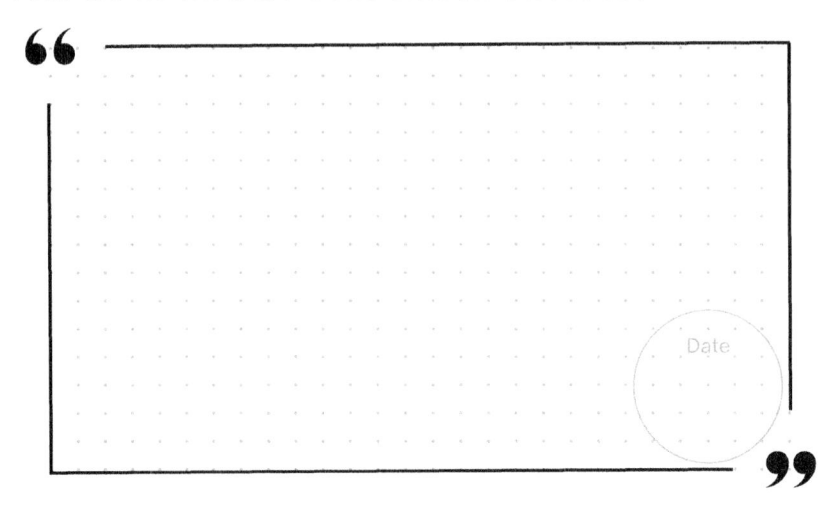

" "

Date

Chapter 42

STOP PICTURING SUCCESS AND DO THIS INSTEAD

- **Redefine Success:** Define success in terms of personal fulfillment rather than external achievements or recognition.
- **Align with Core Values:** Ensure your pursuits align with your deepest values and bring you genuine joy.
- **Embrace the Feeling:** Focus on how success feels personally, not how it appears to others.

WHAT DOES TRUE SUCCESS **FEEL** LIKE TO ME?

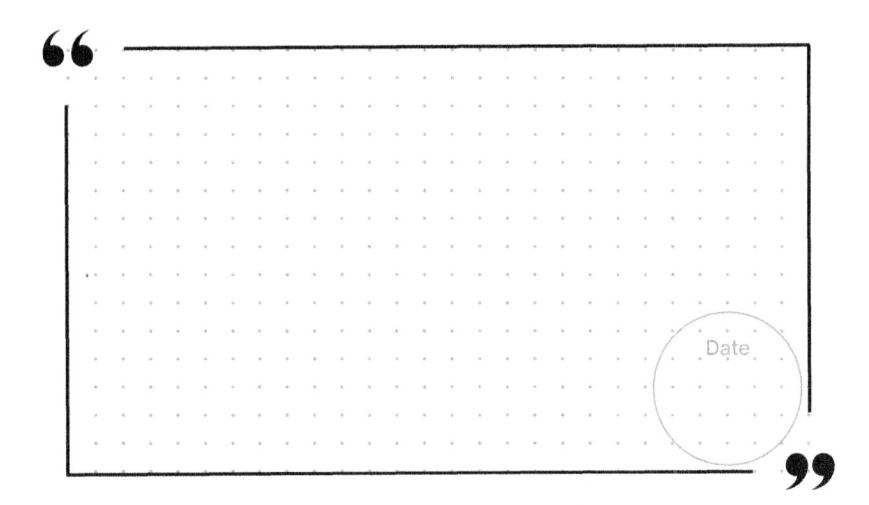

Date

Chapter 43

WHEN YOU THRIVE, EVERYONE WINS

- **Inspire by Example:** Your success can serve as motivation and proof of possibility to others.
- **Share Your Journey:** Openly sharing your challenges and victories can empower and encourage others.
- **Create a Positive Impact:** Use your achievements to make a positive impact in your community and beyond.

HOW CAN MY PERSONAL SUCCESSES SERVE AS INSPIRATION FOR OTHERS, AND WHAT STEPS CAN I TAKE TO SHARE MY JOURNEY MORE OPENLY?

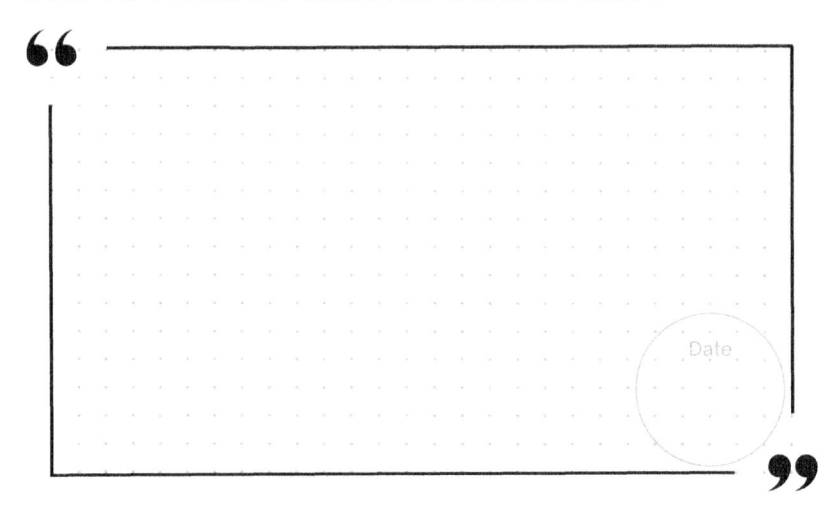

Date

Chapter 44

THE OSCAR CURSE IS REAL

- **Upper Limit Problem:** We often self-sabotage when life exceeds our subconscious threshold of what we believe we deserve.
- **Recognize Self-Sabotage:** Be aware of behaviors that undermine your success when things seem too good.
- **Expand Your Tolerance for Happiness:** Actively work to allow yourself to accept and enjoy greater success and happiness without self-imposed limits.

HOW CAN I RECOGNIZE AND OVERCOME MY OWN UPPER LIMIT PROBLEMS, AND WHERE CAN I ALLOW MYSELF TO EXPERIENCE MORE JOY AND SUCCESS IN MY LIFE?

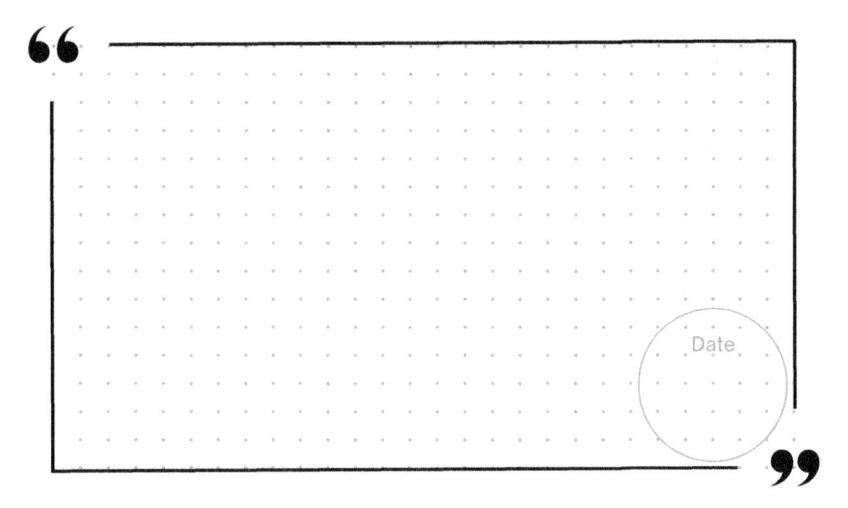

Date

Chapter 45

PAIN IS GOOD BECAUSE IT MAKES YOU MOVE

- **Embrace Adaptability:** Learn to quickly adapt to both positive and negative changes.
- **Maintain Perspective:** Keep a balanced view of life's ups and downs.
- **Cultivate Resilience:** Develop resilience by embracing life's variability and learning from all experiences.

WHERE DO I FEEL A PAIN THAT SHOULD MOTIVATE ME TO TAKE ACTION?

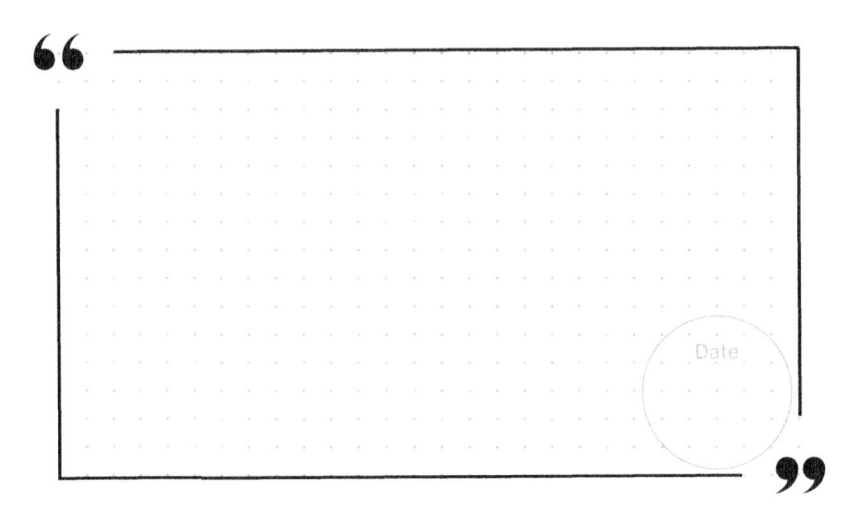

"

Date

"

Chapter 46

COMMITMENT MAKES LIFE EASY - THE 100% RULE

- **Full Commitment Eases Decision-Making:** Fully committing simplifies choices, reducing stress and indecision.
- **100% Commitment Yields Better Results:** Total dedication enhances effectiveness and satisfaction from actions.
- **Identify Areas for Complete Commitment:** Determine which aspects of your life benefit most from undivided attention.

IN WHAT PART OF MY LIFE SHOULD I IMPLEMENT THE 100% RULE TO IMPROVE MY FOCUS AND RESULTS?

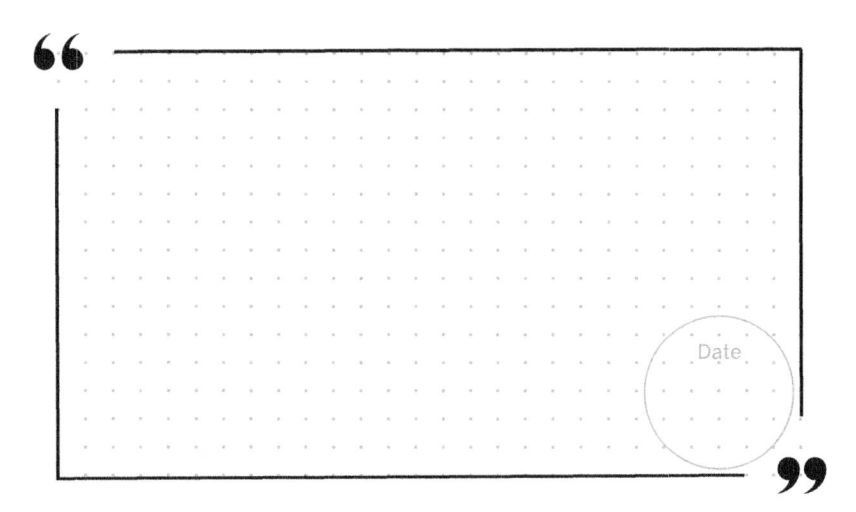

"

Date

"

Chapter 47

LOVING YOU IS THE REAL YOU

- **Release Negative Emotions:** Anger and irritation block creativity and well-being; letting go of these emotions restores inner peace.
- **Choose Love Over Ego:** Recognize that love is your true nature, while negative emotions stem from the ego and distort your reality.
- **Forgiveness as a Path to Freedom:** Forgiving others, and yourself, removes emotional blocks and aligns you with your authentic self.

DO I HAVE ANY ANGER OR FRUSTRATION THAT I CAN LET GO OF TO RECONNECT WITH MY TRUE SELF?

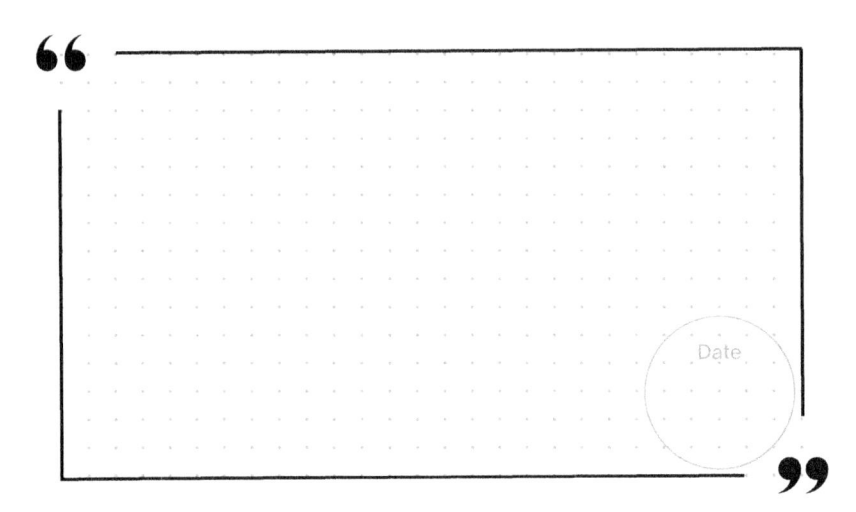

"

Date

"

Chapter 48

WHEN YOU THINK YOU'RE NOT [BLANK] ENOUGH

- **Trust Your Creation:** You were made with unique strengths and capacities—don't argue with the divine design.
- **Use What You Have:** Embrace your attributes and abilities as perfectly suited for your journey.
- **Avoid Limiting Beliefs:** Don't waste energy arguing for perceived limitations; instead, focus on what you can do with what you have.

IF I BELIEVED I WAS ALREADY ENOUGH, WHAT WOULD BE THE FIRST THING I'D DO?

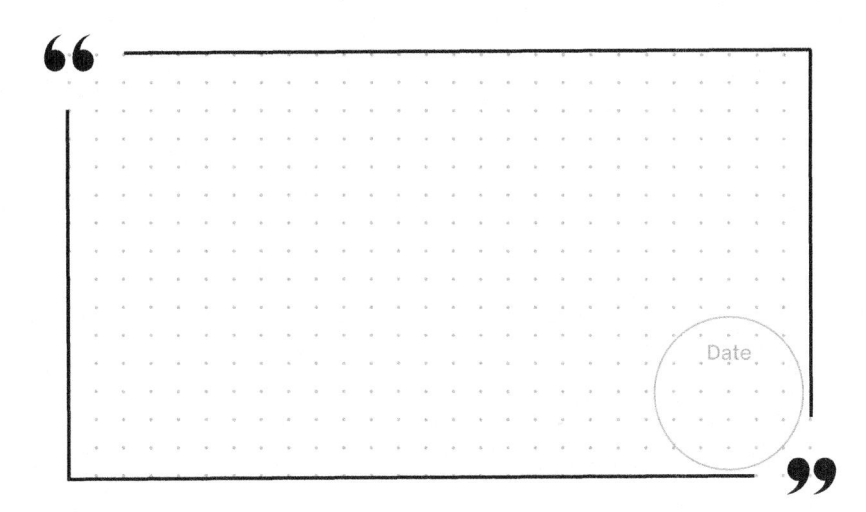

Date

Chapter 49

THE BEST THOUGHTS IGNITE THIS ONE FEELING

- **Thoughts Shape Emotions:** Your thoughts directly influence your emotions, actions, and overall life experience.
- **Embrace Thought Upgrades:** Use negative emotions as signals to consciously choose more soothing and empowering thoughts.
- **Relief is Key:** Seek thoughts that bring a sense of relief to transform stress into calmness and clarity.

WHAT STRESSFUL THOUGHT CAN I REPLACE WITH A MORE SOOTHING, RELIEF-INDUCING THOUGHT RIGHT NOW?

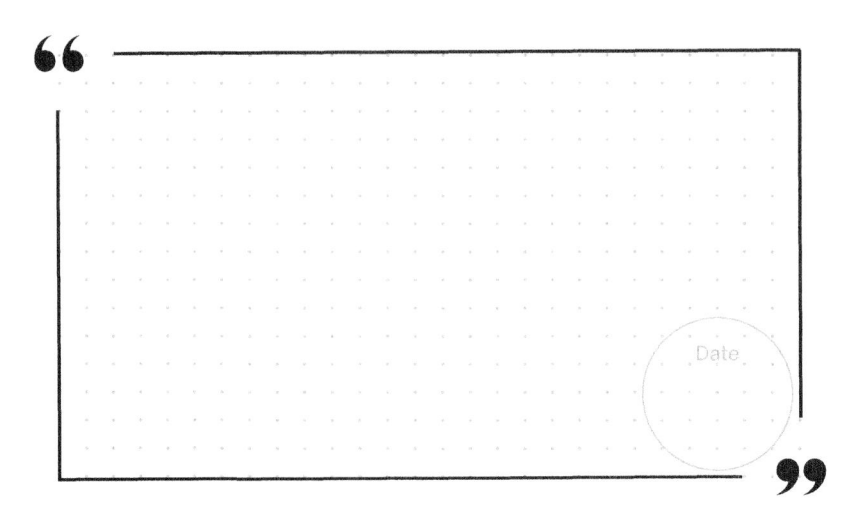

" "

Date

Chapter 50

WHAT PALM TREES TEACH US ABOUT RESILIENCE

- **Flexibility Equals Survival:** Like palm trees in a storm, being flexible allows you to withstand challenges without breaking.
- **Strength Through Adversity:** Difficult experiences can strengthen your foundation, much like storms that deepen palm tree roots.
- **Resilience in Life's Storms:** Embrace life's challenges as opportunities to grow stronger and more resilient.

HOW HAVE THE CHALLENGES I'VE FACED STRENGTHENED ME, AND HOW CAN I BE MORE FLEXIBLE IN THE FACE OF FUTURE ADVERSITY?

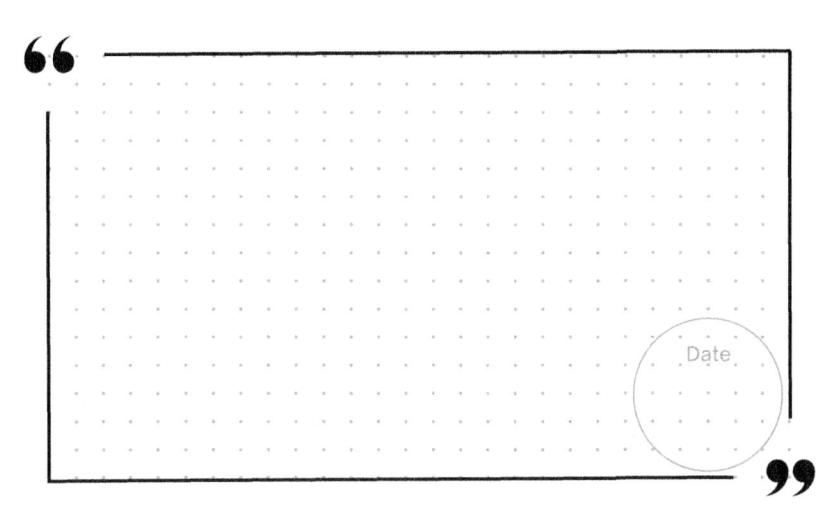

"

Date

"

Chapter 51

WHAT YOU'RE NOT CHANGING, YOU'RE CHOOSING

- **Trust Your Gut**: Decision-making is often about trusting your intuition rather than overanalyzing every option.
- **Inaction is a Choice**: By not making a change, you are actively choosing to stay where you are.
- **Align with Your Decisions**: Once a decision is made, fully commit to it and embrace the outcome.

WHAT AREA OF MY LIFE AM I AVOIDING CHANGE IN, AND HOW CAN I TRUST MY INTUITION TO MAKE A DECISIVE CHOICE?

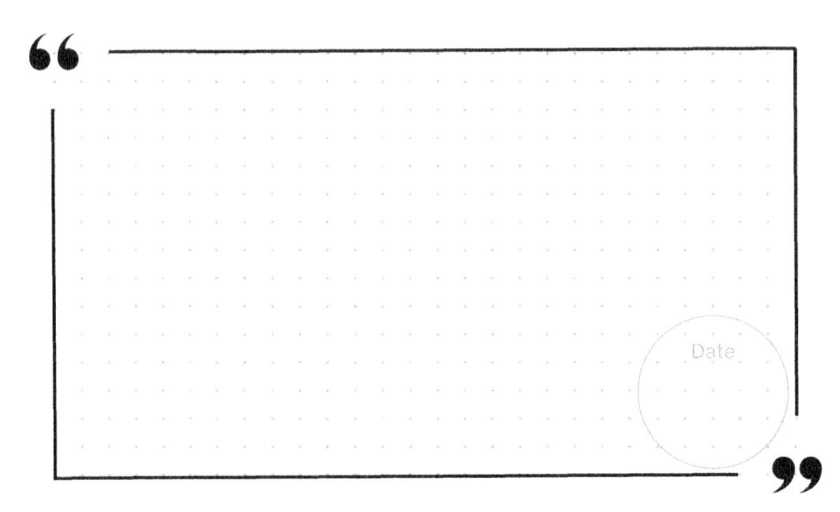

Date

Chapter 52

FUN IS ALWAYS AN OPTION, EVEN WHEN THINGS GO WRONG

- **Choose Fun Over Frustration:** Even in less-than-ideal circumstances, you can choose to make the best of the situation by having fun.
- **Adapt to Challenges:** Instead of complaining, adapt to the situation and find joy in simple moments.
- **Mindset Matters:** Your attitude and perspective can turn mundane or challenging situations into enjoyable experiences.

IN WHICH SITUATIONS CAN I CHOOSE TO ADD MORE FUN IN THE FUTURE, AND HOW?

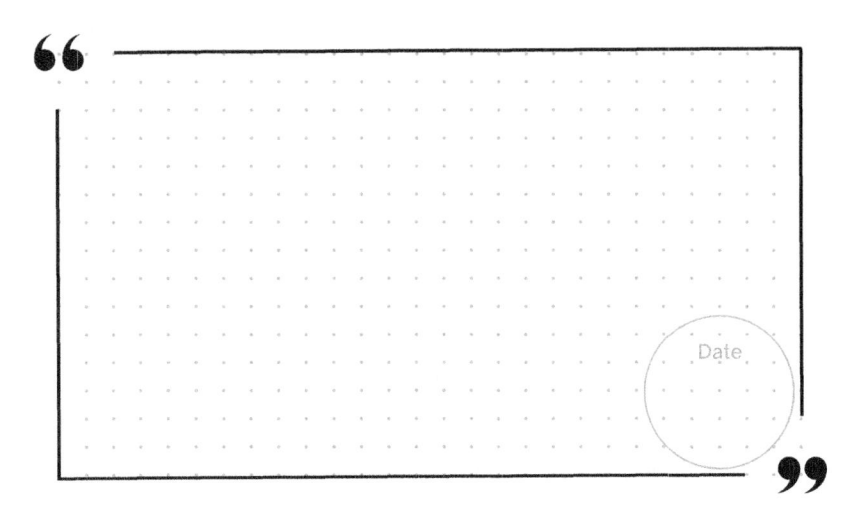

Date

Chapter 53

DON'T ROB YOURSELF OF NEW EXPERIENCES

- **Embrace Experience Over Observation:** True growth and fulfillment come from actively participating in life, not just observing it.
- **Small Wins Lead to Success:** Success is built on a series of small experiences and wins accumulated over time.
- **Live Boldly:** Take risks and pursue your own journey rather than just admiring others' experiences from afar.

IN WHAT AREAS OF MY LIFE AM I OBSERVING RATHER THAN EXPERIENCING, AND HOW CAN I ACTIVELY ENGAGE MORE?

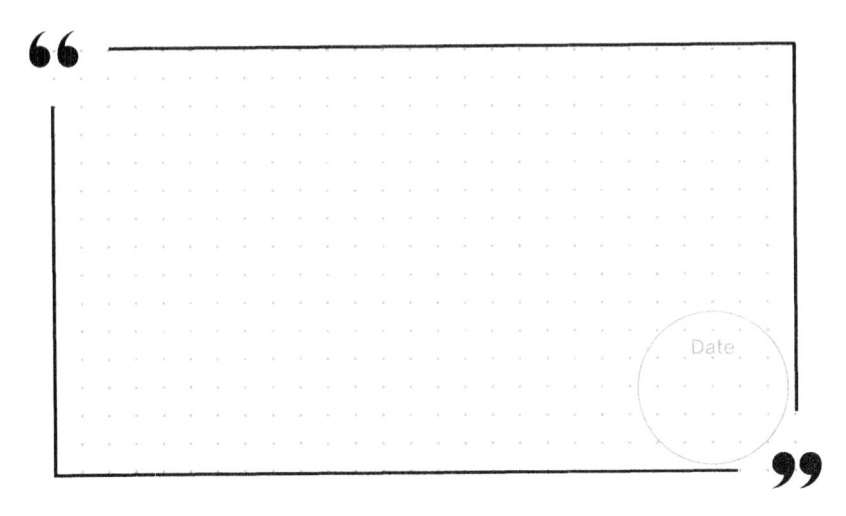

Chapter 54

WE ARE EVERYTHING WE SEE AND FEEL

- **Reflective Relationships:** The traits you admire or dislike in others are reflections of qualities within yourself.
- **Triggers as Opportunities:** When someone frustrates you, it's a chance to identify and heal parts of yourself that need attention.
- **Self-Awareness:** Recognizing that how you see the world is a reflection of your inner state can lead to personal growth.

WHO IN MY LIFE IS TRIGGERING ME RIGHT NOW, AND WHAT DOES THIS REVEAL ABOUT AREAS WITHIN MYSELF THAT NEED HEALING OR TRANSFORMATION?

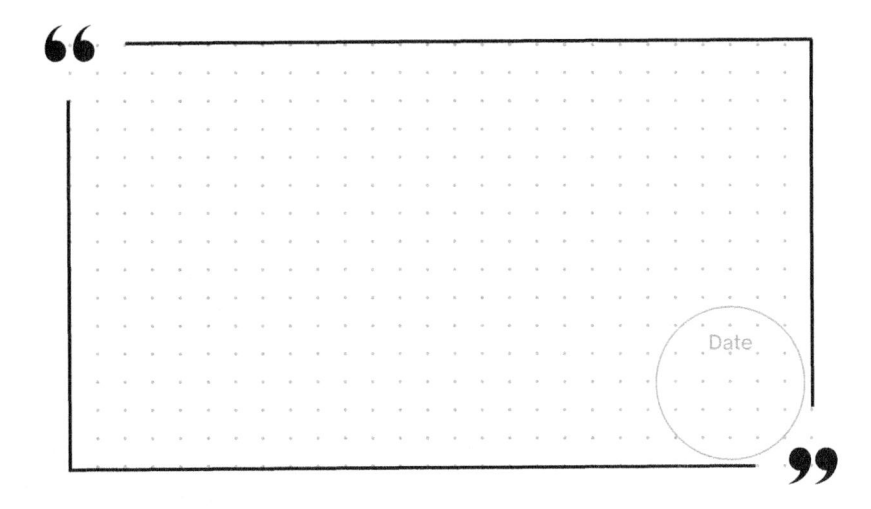

"

Date

"

Chapter 55

THE WORLD WILL ALWAYS MATCH YOUR ENERGY

- **Energy Influence:** Your energy directly impacts those around you, shaping the mood and interactions.
- **Self-Responsibility:** Be mindful of the energy you bring into any space, as it sets the tone for the environment.
- **Reflective Relationships:** Others will often mirror the energy you project, so choose to lead with positivity and openness.

HOW CAN I BE MORE MINDFUL OF THE ENERGY I BRING INTO MY INTERACTIONS, AND WHAT STEPS CAN I TAKE TO ENSURE IT'S POSITIVE?

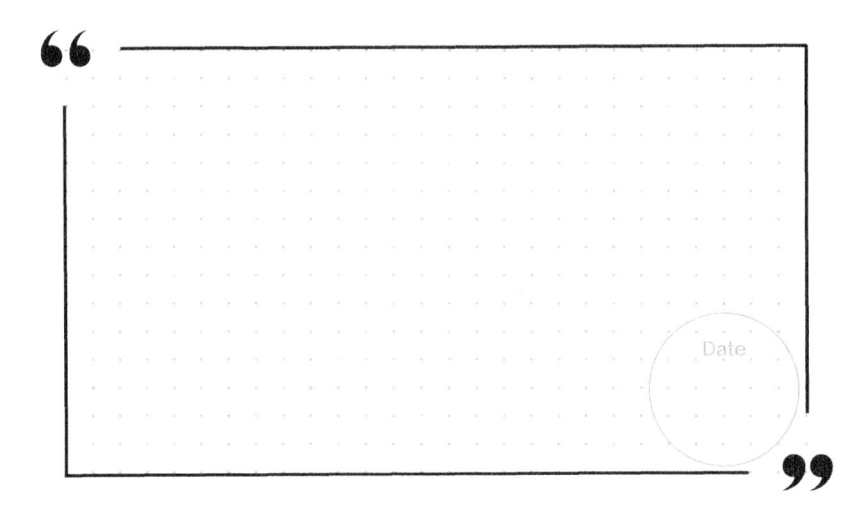

"

Date

"

Chapter 56

SAVING MONEY IS EXPENSIVE SOMETIMES

- **Avoid False Economy:** Trying to save money by doing everything yourself can lead to greater costs in terms of time, energy and quality.
- **Invest Wisely:** Consider where spending money could actually save you time and stress, leading to better outcomes.
- **Value Your Time:** Remember that time is a non-renewable resource—sometimes, it's worth paying more to preserve it.

WHERE IN MY LIFE AM I TRYING TO SAVE MONEY AT THE EXPENSE OF MY TIME AND WELL-BEING, AND HOW CAN I MAKE BETTER CHOICES?

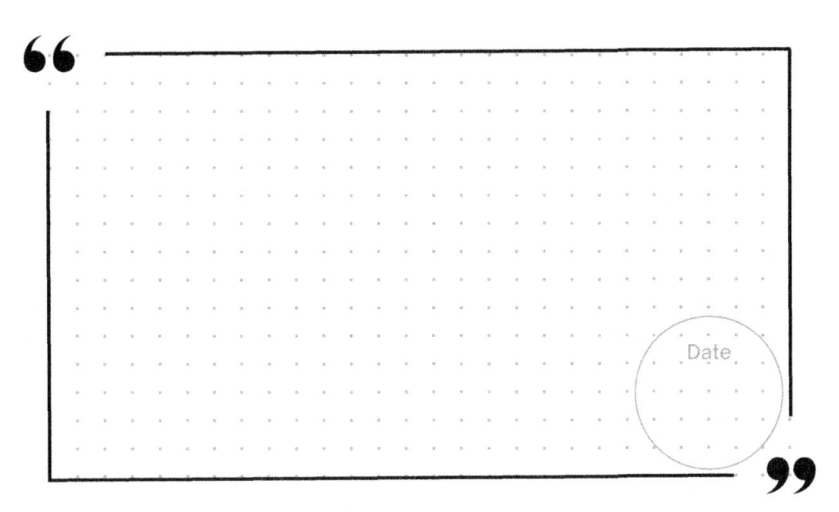

Date

Chapter 57

JUST BE ON TIME

- **Punctuality Reduces Stress:** Being on time helps you avoid anxiety and the need to apologize constantly.
- **Respect for Others:** Timeliness shows respect for other people's time and efforts.
- **Simple Organization:** Being punctual is a straightforward way to demonstrate that you are organized and reliable.

HOW CAN I IMPROVE MY PUNCTUALITY TO REDUCE STRESS AND SHOW MORE RESPECT FOR OTHERS' TIME?

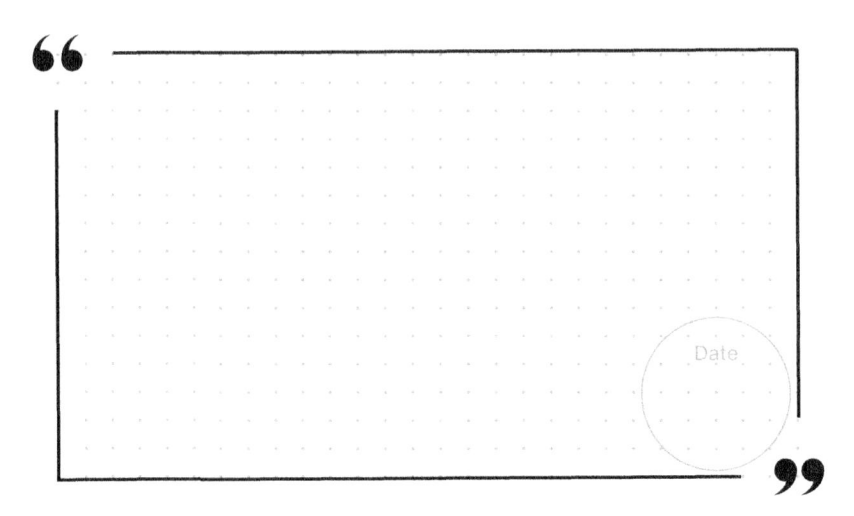

Date

Chapter 58

DON'T UNDERESTIMATE YOUR CONTRIBUTION

- **Value Your Work:** Just because your work feels enjoyable or easy doesn't mean it isn't valuable and deserving of compensation.
- **Recognize Your Efforts:** Acknowledge the effort and time you put into your work, even if it feels second nature to you.
- **Combat Imposter Syndrome:** Don't let self-doubt diminish the worth of your contributions—recognize and assert your value.

WHERE AM I CONTRIBUTING MORE THAN I AM GETTING CREDIT FOR, AND HOW CAN I ADDRESS THIS?

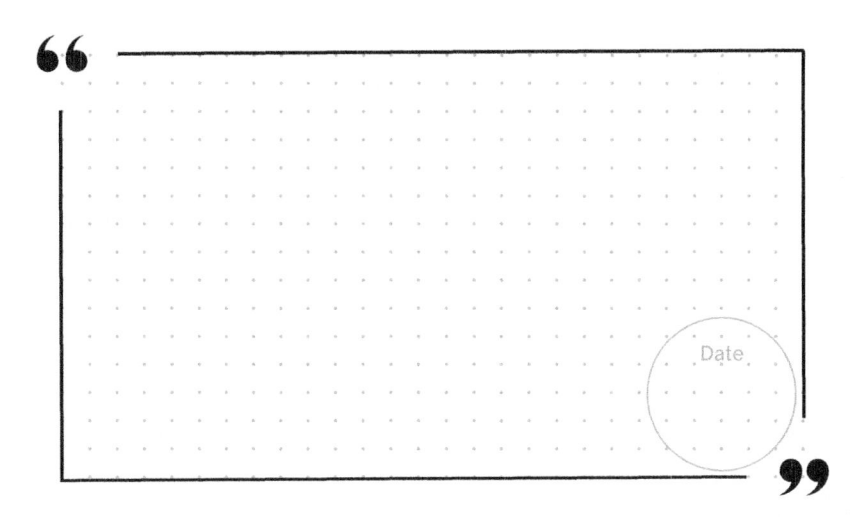

"

Date

"

Chapter 59

BOREDOM IS DANGEROUS

- **Idle Minds Can Drift Negatively:** Boredom can lead to unproductive thoughts and negativity if not consciously managed.
- **Stay Engaged:** Keeping yourself busy with meaningful activities helps maintain focus and happiness.
- **Progress Equals Happiness:** Actively engaging in life and pursuing progress leads to greater fulfillment and well-being.

WHERE IS BOREDOM SHOWING UP IN MY LIFE, AND HOW CAN I FILL THAT TIME WITH ACTIVITIES THAT BRING ME JOY AND PROGRESS?

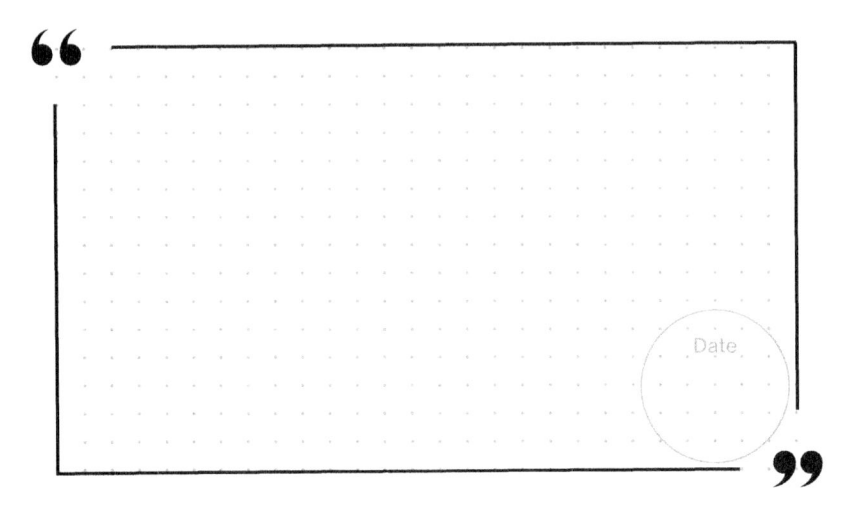

"

Date

"

Chapter 60

IT'S ALL RELATIVE

- **Perspective Shapes Reality:** Everyone sees the world differently based on their unique experiences and context.
- **Embrace Relativity:** Understanding that truth is relative allows you to be more accepting of others' viewpoints and choices.
- **Let Go of Absolutes:** There is no one 'right' way to live—accepting this leads to a more peaceful and easygoing life.

HOW CAN I BE MORE OPEN TO DIFFERING PERSPECTIVES AND LET GO OF THE NEED TO PROVE MY WAY IS THE 'RIGHT' WAY?

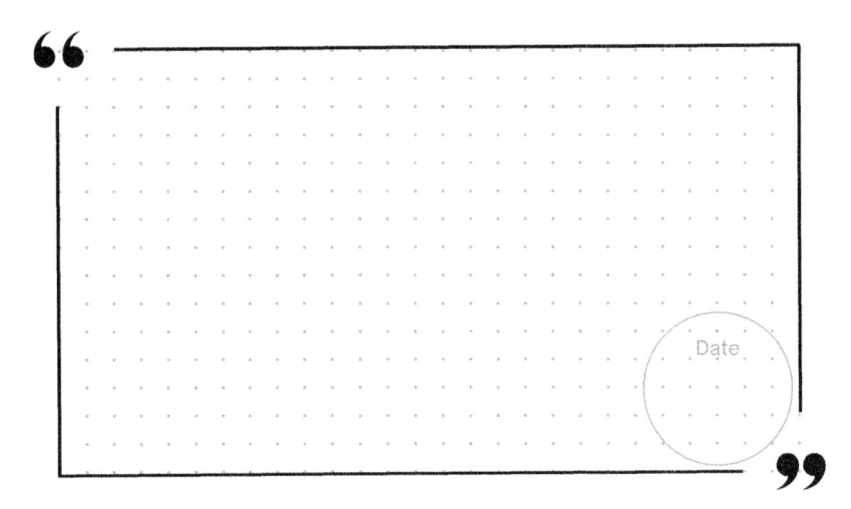

Date

Chapter 61

NO ONE INTENDS TO SCREW UP THEIR LIFE

- **Compassion Over Judgment:** Understand that people make mistakes not because they choose harm, but because they seek relief or happiness in misguided ways.
- **Acceptance of Differences:** Recognizing that everyone has their own ways of coping can help you be more forgiving and compassionate.
- **Love as a Guiding Principle:** Approaching others with love, even when it's difficult, is often the best way to navigate challenging relationships.

WHO IN MY LIFE DO I NEED TO LOVE MORE INSTEAD OF TRYING TO FIX?

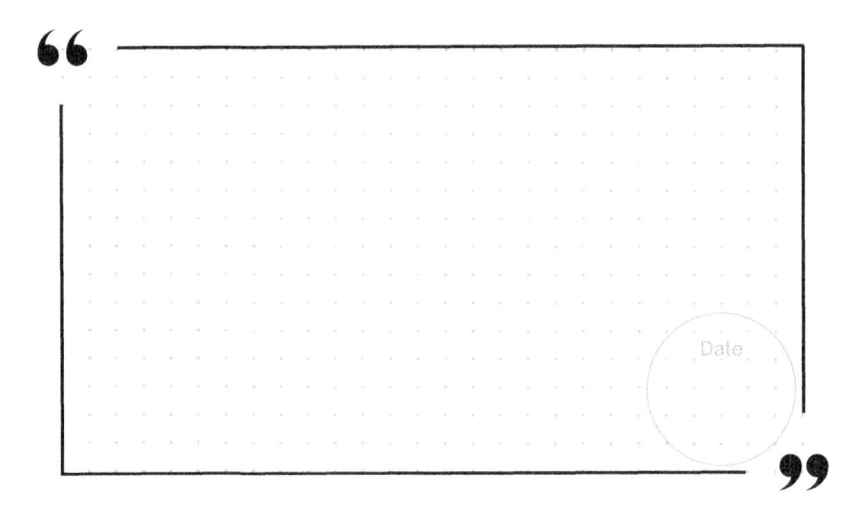

"

Date

"

Chapter 62

GOOD ENOUGH IS

- **Perfectionism Limits Potential:** Striving for perfection often means you're only operating at a fraction of your potential.
- **Action Over Perfection:** Aim for excellence and take action, even if it's not perfect, progress is more valuable than unattainable perfection.
- **Embrace Imperfection:** Accept that 'good enough' can lead to fruitful results, much like a thriving garden that grows beyond expectations.

WHERE IN MY LIFE CAN I EMBRACE 'GOOD ENOUGH' AND FOCUS ON TAKING ACTION INSTEAD OF STRIVING FOR PERFECTION?

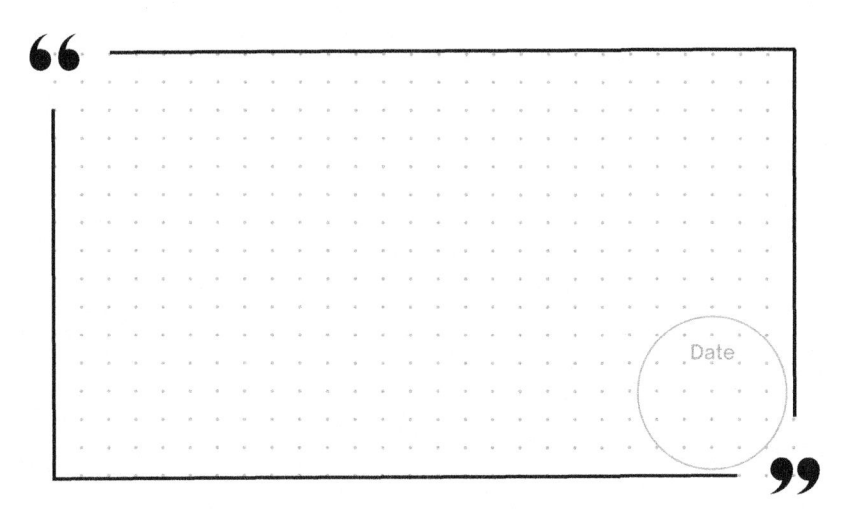

Date

Chapter 63

TELL PEOPLE WHO ARE SUFFERING THEY'RE NOT ALONE

- **Acknowledge Struggles:** Letting someone know that they are not alone in their suffering can provide immense comfort and support.
- **Presence is Powerful:** Sometimes, just being there for someone, even in silence, can be a profound act of love.
- **Express Empathy:** Simple gestures like a heartfelt note can have a lasting impact, showing care and understanding.

WHO IN MY LIFE MIGHT BE FEELING ALONE RIGHT NOW, AND HOW CAN I LET THEM KNOW THAT I'M HERE FOR THEM?

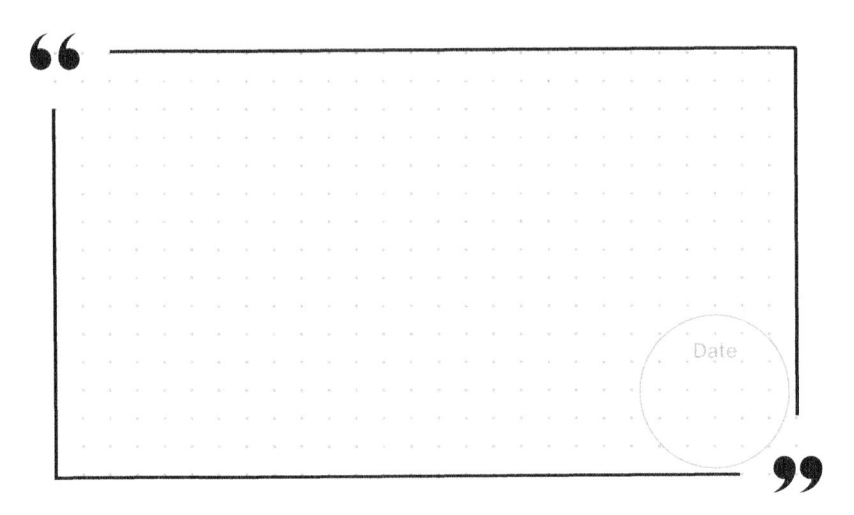

Date

Chapter 64

COUPLES THERAPY: JUST DO IT

- **Value of Communication:** Open communication facilitated by therapy, can help couples understand each other and address underlying issues.
- **Different Perspectives:** Therapy can reveal new ways of seeing your partner's behavior and motivations, fostering mutual appreciation.
- **Prevention Over Cure:** Addressing relationship challenges early through therapy can prevent bigger issues down the line.

WHAT WOULD I MOST LIKE MY PARTNER TO KNOW RIGHT NOW, AND HOW CAN I COMMUNICATE IT IN A SUPPORTIVE WAY?

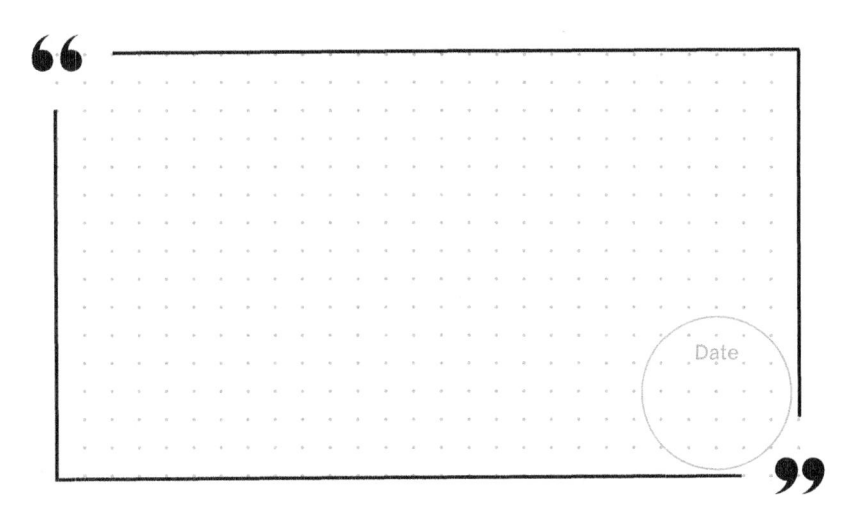

"

Date

"

Chapter 65

UNMUTE YOURSELF

- **Power of Sharing:** Opening up about personal struggles can provide comfort and support to others who may be facing similar challenges.
- **Breaking Isolation:** Sharing your experiences helps others feel less alone and more connected.
- **Be Generous with Your Story:** While privacy is important, sharing what has worked for you can be a gift to those in need of reassurance.

WHERE AM I HOLDING BACK FROM HELPING OTHERS, AND HOW CAN I OVERCOME MY FEAR TO OFFER SUPPORT?

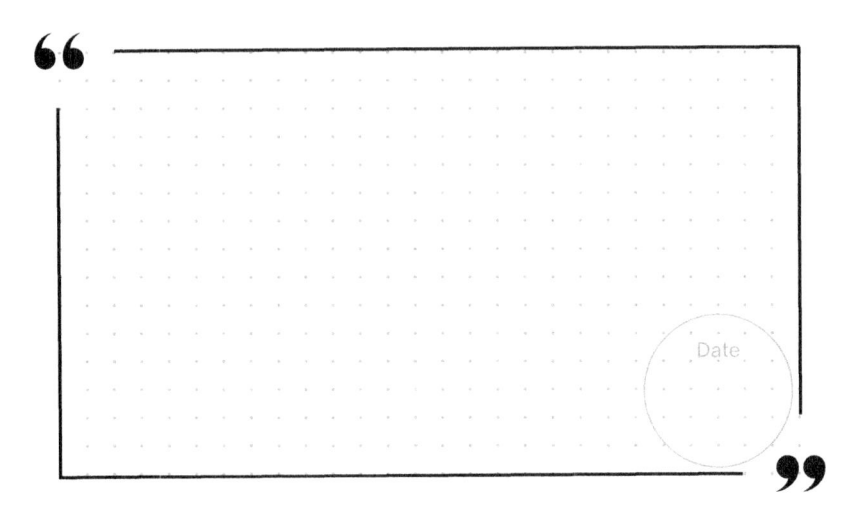

Date

Chapter 66

THE PRESENT MOMENT CREATES THE PAST

- **Power of Perspective:** The way you choose to remember and tell your past story shapes your current reality.
- **Rewrite Your Narrative:** You have the ability to change your personal story by focusing on the aspects that empower you.
- **Selective Memory:** The memories you choose to focus on and repeat to yourself will become your truth.

HOW CAN I RESHAPE MY PAST BY CHOOSING TO FOCUS ON THE MEMORIES AND STORIES THAT EMPOWER ME?

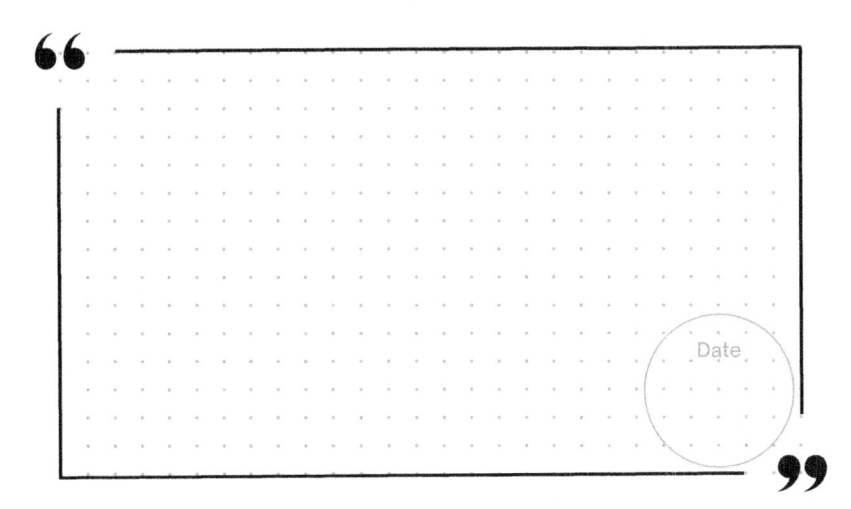

"

Date

"

Chapter 67

DON'T DEPRIVE OTHERS OF THE JOY OF HELPING YOU

- **Let Others Help:** Allowing others to assist you not only helps you but also gives them the joy of being of service.
- **Value of Receiving:** Receiving help can strengthen your bonds with others and remind you of your worth.
- **Ask for Support:** When you're stuck, don't hesitate to reach out—help is often closer than you think.

WHERE IN MY LIFE AM I HESITANT TO ASK FOR HELP, AND HOW CAN I OPEN MYSELF UP TO RECEIVING SUPPORT?

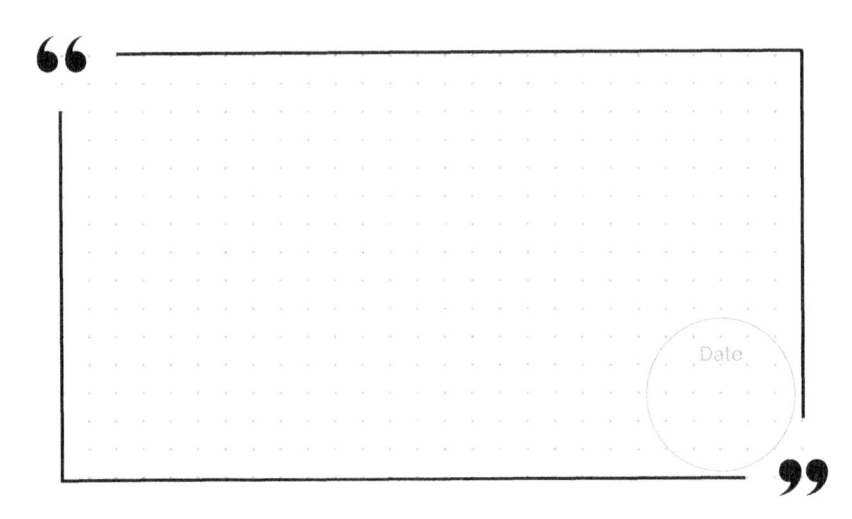

Date

Chapter 68

PUTTING YOURSELF FIRST IS GENEROUS

- **Self-Care Benefits Others:** Taking care of yourself ensures you have the energy and positivity to give to others.
- **Quality Over Quantity:** When you're well-rested and happy, you can contribute more meaningfully and authentically.
- **Redefine Self-Care:** Self-care isn't about luxury; it's about making choices that keep you nourished and balanced.

HOW CAN I BETTER PRIORITIZE MY OWN NEEDS SO THAT I CAN SHOW UP MORE FULLY FOR OTHERS?

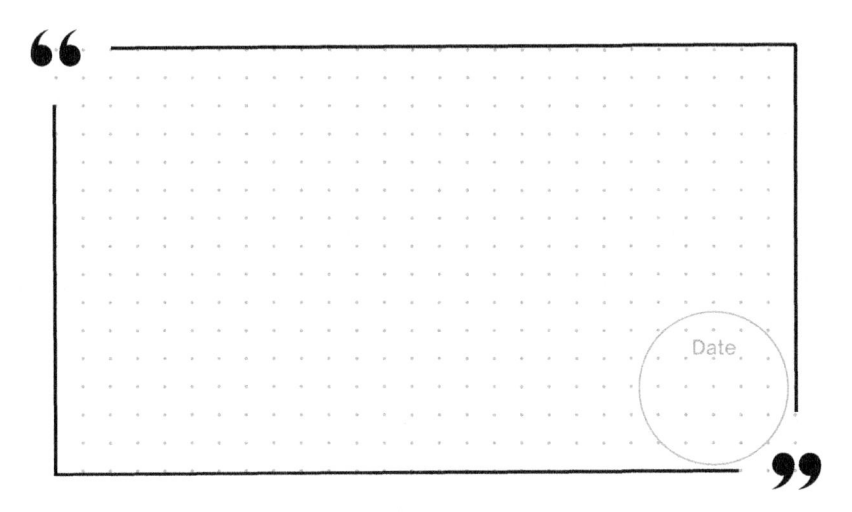

"

Date

"

Chapter 69

A SECRET SUPERPOWER

- **Conscious Awareness:** Recognizing your habitual reactions allows you to choose a more mindful response.
- **Separate Stimulus and Response:** Being aware of the gap between an external event and your reaction is a powerful tool for emotional control.
- **Practice Mindful Observation:** By observing your impulses before acting, you can maintain calm and avoid unnecessary conflict.

IN WHAT SITUATIONS CAN I PRACTICE OBSERVING MY REACTIONS BEFORE RESPONDING, AND HOW MIGHT THIS CHANGE MY INTERACTIONS?

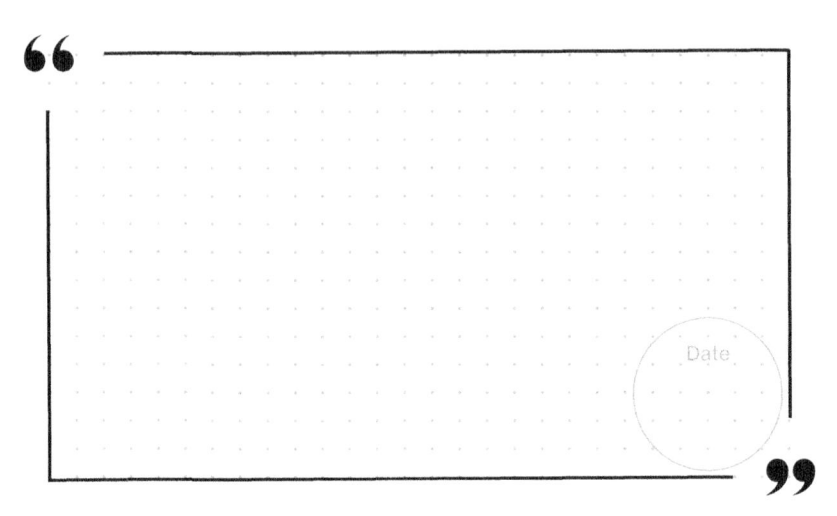

Chapter 70

DON'T JUST CONSUME, CREATE

- **Balance Creation and Consumption:** Strive for a 50-50 balance between creating content and consuming it to stay engaged and purposeful online.
- **Be an Active Participant:** Engaging with social media as a creator rather than just a consumer leads to a more fulfilling experience.
- **Take Breaks:** Periodic breaks from social media can help you reconnect with your own values and reduce reliance on external validation.

WHERE IN MY LIFE CAN I FOCUS MORE ON CREATING RATHER THAN CONSUMING?

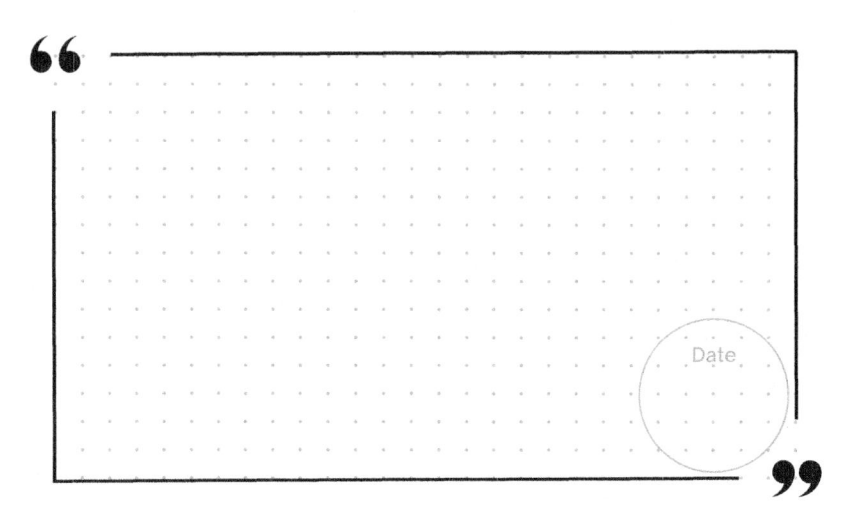

"

Date

"

Chapter 71

TALK ABOUT IT ALREADY

- **Discuss Life Priorities:** Align on key life goals like travel, career, and family to ensure you and your partner are heading in the same direction.
- **Financial Transparency:** Address financial expectations and responsibilities early to avoid future conflicts.
- **Prepare for the Future:** Conversations about children, family roles, and long-term commitments are crucial for a harmonious relationship.

WHERE DO I NEED TO INITIATE IMPORTANT CONVERSATIONS IN MY RELATIONSHIPS TO ENSURE LONG-TERM ALIGNMENT AND EASE?

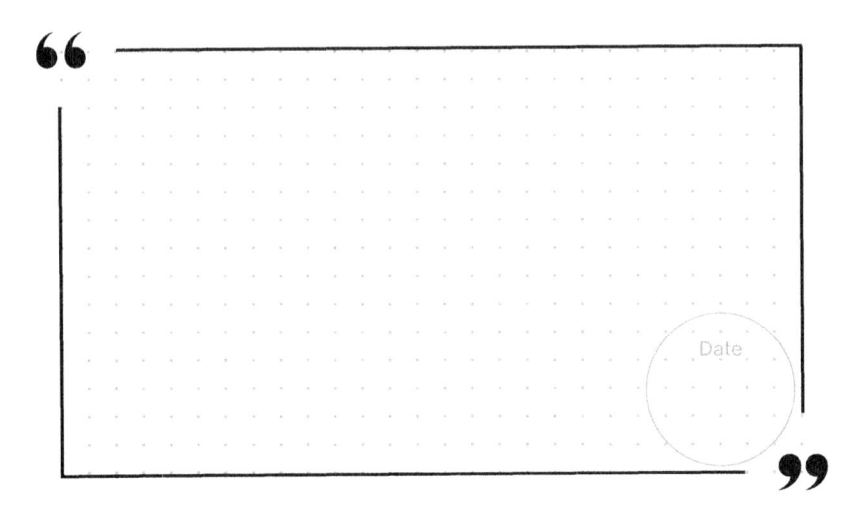

" "

Date

Chapter 72

STOP FIGHTING WITH YOURSELF

- **Mind-Body Connection:** The language we use about our bodies impacts our health and well-being. Opt for positive, healing language.
- **Ease Over Conflict:** Shift from battle-focused language to words that promote healing and peace.
- **Focus on Positives:** Whether in health or relationships, focusing on what you love and appreciate can transform your experience.

WHERE IN MY LIFE CAN I REPLACE CONFLICT-FOCUSED LANGUAGE WITH WORDS OF HEALING AND EASE?

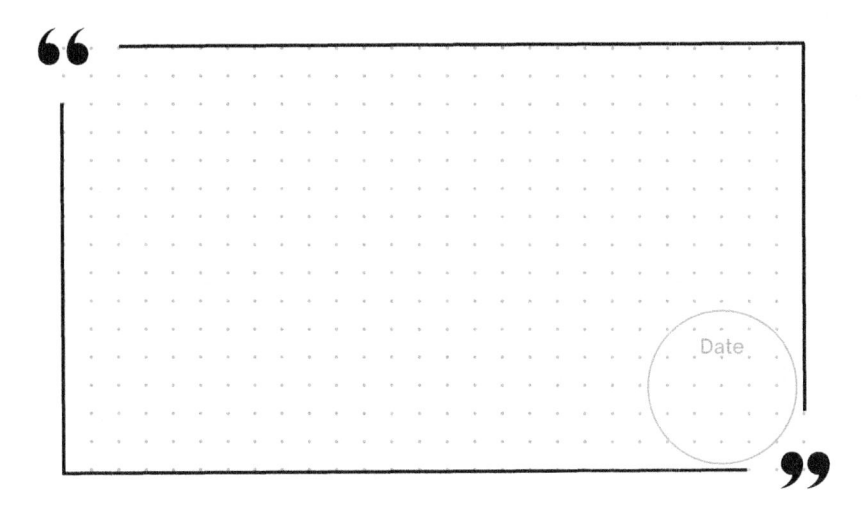

"

Date

"

Chapter 73

AUSTRALIAN WISDOM YOU CAN USE EVERY DAY

- **No Worries Attitude:** Adopting a 'no worries' mindset can reduce unnecessary stress and anxiety.
- **Worry vs. Action:** Worrying doesn't solve problems—taking positive action does.
- **Mind Management:** You're in charge of your thoughts; choose to focus on what you can control and let go of the rest.

HOW CAN I ADOPT A 'NO WORRIES' MINDSET IN AREAS WHERE I TEND TO OVERTHINK?

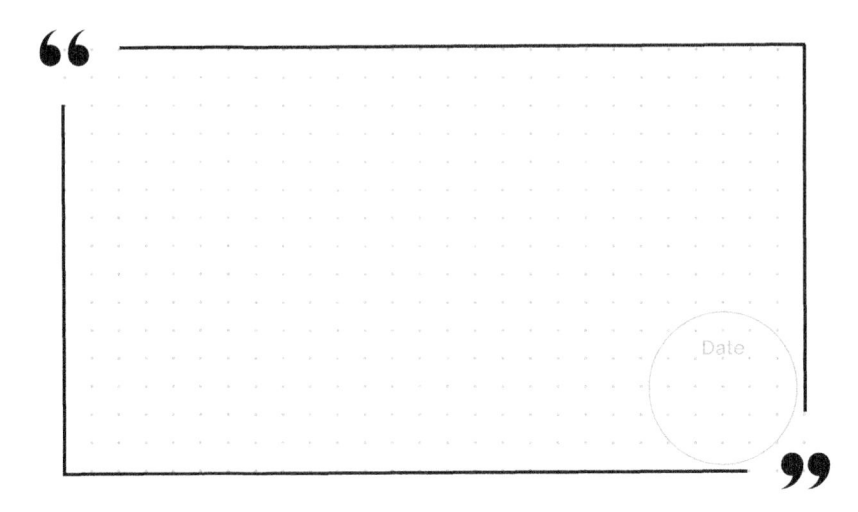

"

Date

"

Chapter 74

SUCCESS LEAVES CLUES

- **Self-Reflection:** Your true passions and purpose are often revealed through your everyday interests and actions.
- **Guided Journaling:** Asking yourself specific questions can help uncover what truly excites and motivates you.
- **Simplicity in Clarity:** Don't overthink; clarity often comes when you allow yourself to relax and reflect.

WHAT DO I FEEL IS THE TRUE PASSION OF MY LIFE?

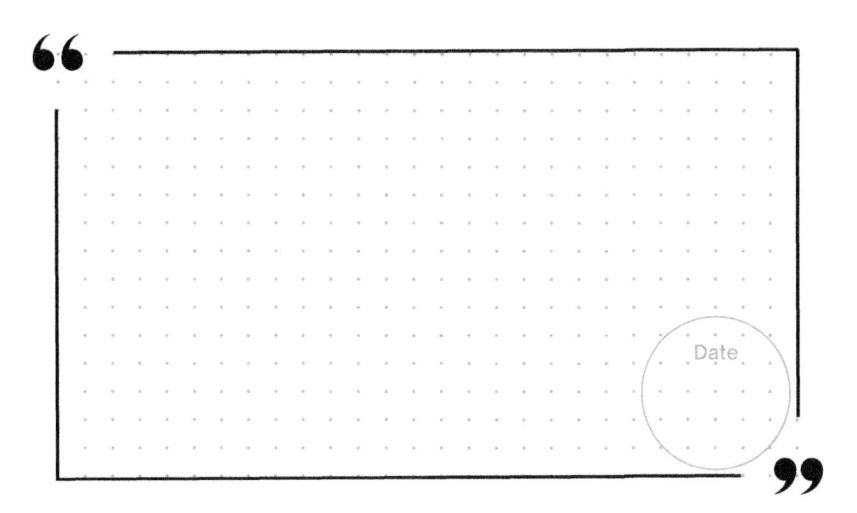

"

Date

"

Finding My Path

> **WHAT DO I DO WHEN I SLACK OFF AT WORK?**
>
> Date

> **WHAT BLOGS AND BOOKS DO I LOVE?**
>
> Date

Finding My Path

> **WHO WOULD I LOVE TO BE FOR A WEEK?**
>
> *Date*

> **WHAT AM I LEAST INSECURE ABOUT?**
>
> *Date*

Finding My Path

> **WHAT'S PURE FUN FOR ME?**
>
> *Date*

> **WHAT TOPIC NEVER GETS BORING FOR ME?**
>
> *Date*

Finding My Path

" WHAT PEOPLE DO I FEEL MOST AT EASE WITH?

Date

"

" WITHOUT OVERTHINKING: MY PATH IN LIFE IS...

Date

"

Chapter 75

HOW TO GIVE THE PERFECT GIFT

- **Consider the Recipient's Preferences:** The perfect gift aligns with what the recipient values, not what you might love to receive.
- **Avoid Assumptions:** Don't assume others share your tastes or priorities; instead, focus on what would make them truly happy.
- **Ask for Input:** To ensure your gift is well-received, simply ask the person what they would like or need.

WHO IN MY LIFE DO I NEED TO ASK ABOUT THEIR PREFERENCES TO GIVE THEM A MORE THOUGHTFUL GIFT?

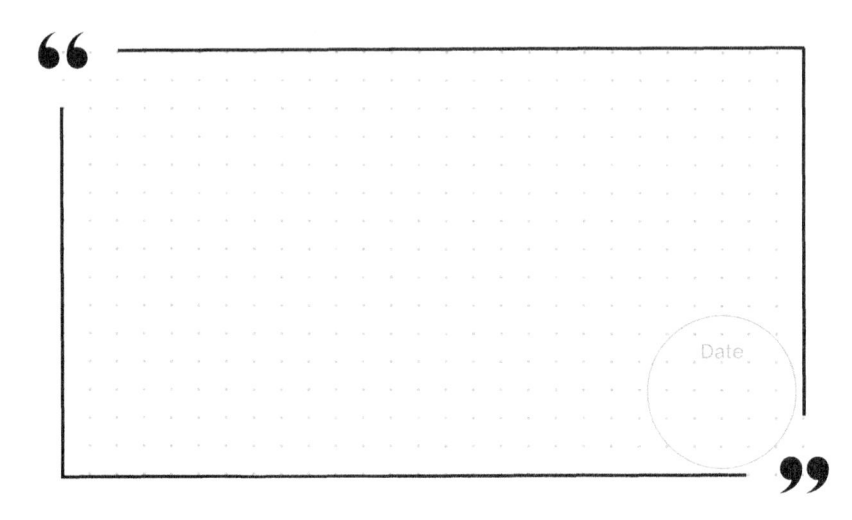

Chapter 76

YOU SPOT IT, YOU GOT IT

- **Perception Reflection:** We notice in the world what we hold within ourselves—beauty, pain, or otherwise.
- **Self-Insight:** What you see in others often reveals truths about yourself.
- **Empathy and Understanding:** Recognize that others' reactions are a reflection of their inner state, not necessarily a judgment of you.

WHAT DO I TEND TO NOTICE THE MOST, AND WHAT DOES THIS REVEAL ABOUT MY OWN INNER STATE?

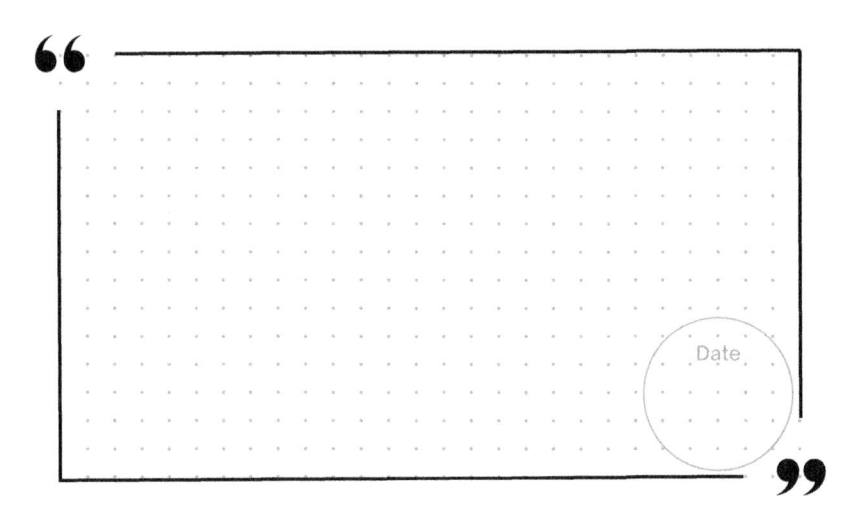

> " "

Date

Chapter 77

A POSITIVE MENTAL ATTITUDE CAN SAVE A LIFE

- **Influence of Belief:** Positive thinking can dramatically change outcomes.
- **Impact of Care:** Persistent support can lead to remarkable recoveries.
- **Adopted Children's Needs:** They need emotional reassurance and validation.

WHERE DO I SEE POSSIBILITIES THAT OTHERS MIGHT OVERLOOK, AND HOW CAN I EMBRACE AND ACT ON THEM?

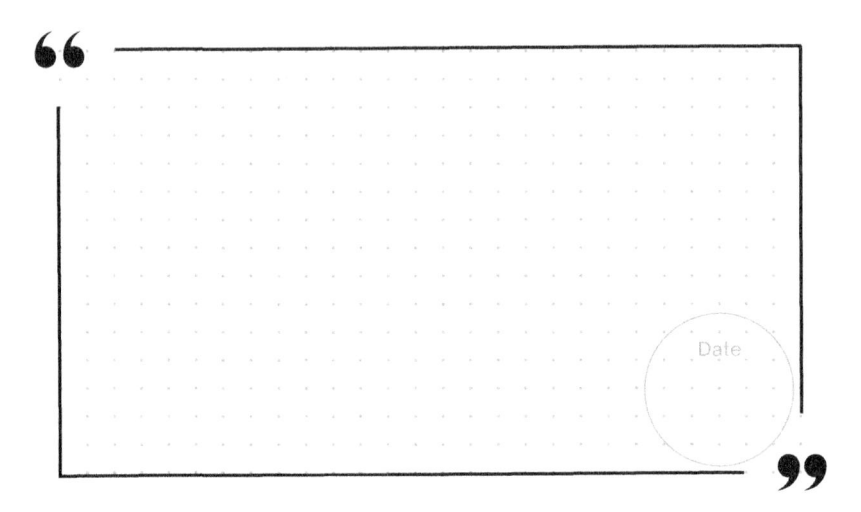

Date

Chapter 78

YOUR VALUE IS NOT DETERMINED BY HOW OTHER PEOPLE TREAT YOU

- **Intrinsic Worth:** Your value is inherent and not affected by others' opinions or approval.
- **Unique Significance:** Every individual is unique and valuable simply by being themselves, regardless of external validation.
- **Consistent Value:** Just like a $100 bill, your worth remains unchanged despite external circumstances or treatment.

IN WHAT AREAS OF MY LIFE DO I ALLOW OTHERS' OPINIONS TO INFLUENCE MY SENSE OF SELF-WORTH, AND HOW CAN I REMIND MYSELF OF MY INHERENT VALUE?

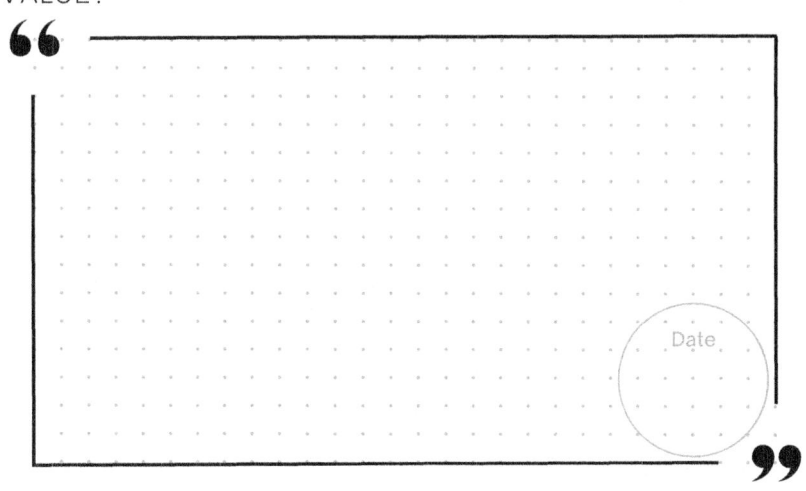

Chapter 79

SOMEONE'S DEATH DOES NOT DEFINE THEIR LIFE

- **Beyond the End:** A person's worth is defined by their life and character, not by the manner or timing of their death.
- **Celebrate Life:** It's important to remember and celebrate the positive and unique qualities of those we've lost.
- **True Remembrance:** Focus on the entirety of a person's life, not just the final chapter.

HOW CAN I BETTER CELEBRATE AND REMEMBER THE POSITIVE QUALITIES OF PEOPLE I'VE LOST, RATHER THAN FOCUSING ON THE CIRCUMSTANCES OF THEIR PASSING?

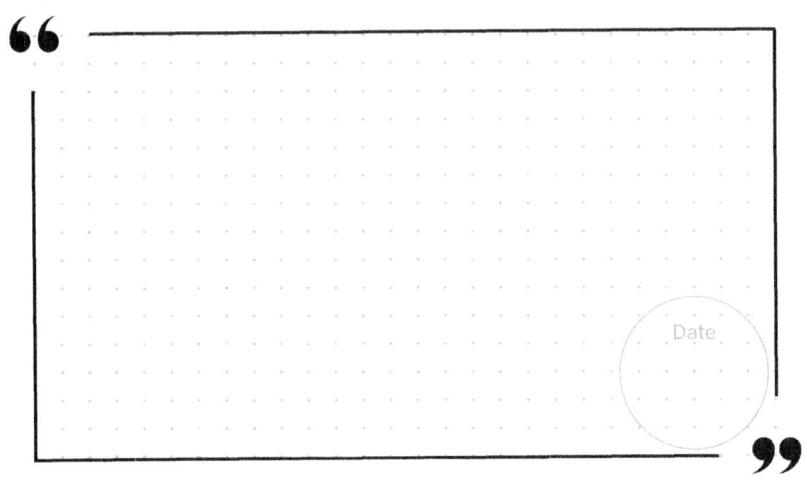

Date

Chapter 80

IT'S OKAY TO BREAK UP WITH A FRIEND

- **Natural Drift:** Friendships can change as life evolves, and that's okay.
- **Personal Growth:** As you grow, you may attract people who better match your current self.
- **Gentle Shift:** It's fine to gradually change the dynamics of a friendship without feeling guilty.

HOW HAVE MY FRIENDSHIPS CHANGED WITH MY PERSONAL GROWTH, AND HOW CAN I ACCEPT THESE CHANGES WITHOUT GUILT?

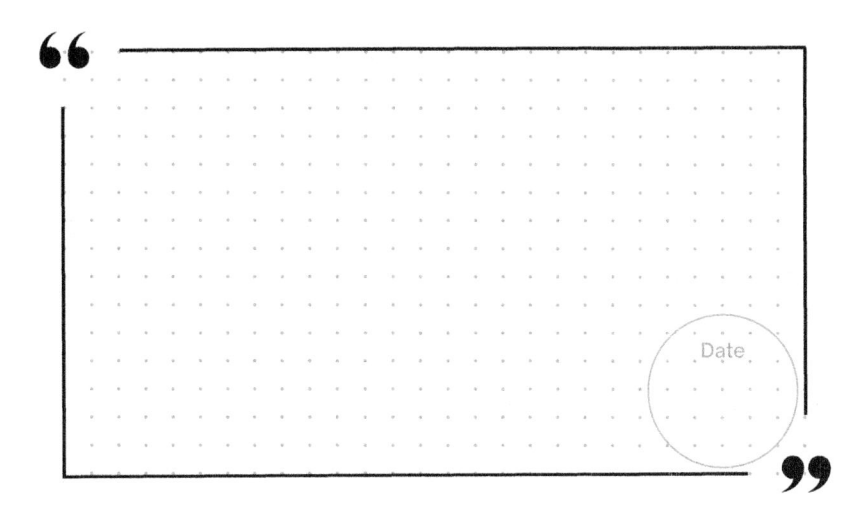

"

Date

"

Chapter 81

LET'S REVEL IN YOUR ACCOMPLISHMENTS FOR A SECOND

- **Celebrate Achievements:** Pause to acknowledge and celebrate even small victories.
- **Appreciate Progress:** Recognize how much you've achieved over the past year.
- **Value Personal Wins:** Appreciate both visible and private achievements.

HOW CAN I CELEBRATE MY RECENT ACCOMPLISHMENTS AND ACKNOWLEDGE MY PROGRESS, BOTH BIG AND SMALL?

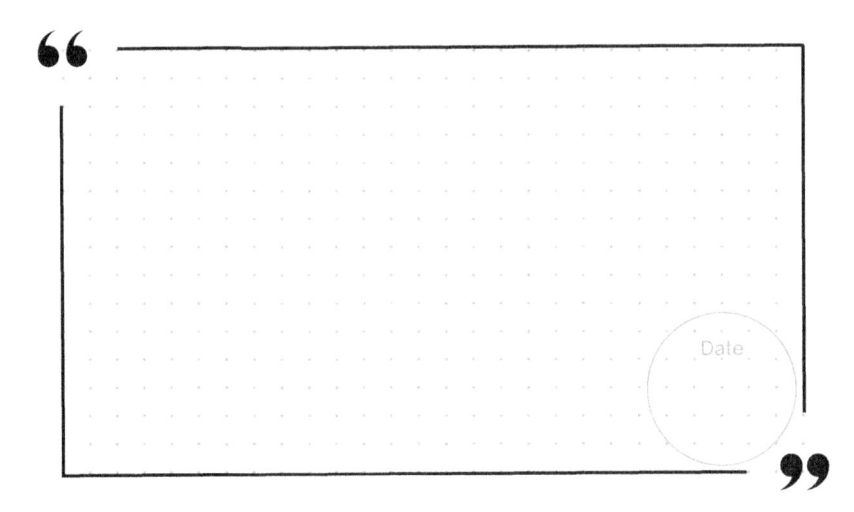

"

Date

"

Chapter 82

CAN'T FORGIVE? THAT'S UNDERSTANDABLE

- **Understand Your Feelings:** It's natural to struggle with forgiveness after being deeply hurt.
- **Assess the Relationship:** Evaluate if the person who hurt you is committed to genuine change.
- **Forgiveness and Boundaries:** If you choose to forgive, focus on moving forward without constantly revisiting the hurt.

IS THERE SOMEONE OR SOMETHING I WISH TO FORGIVE AND LET GO OF?

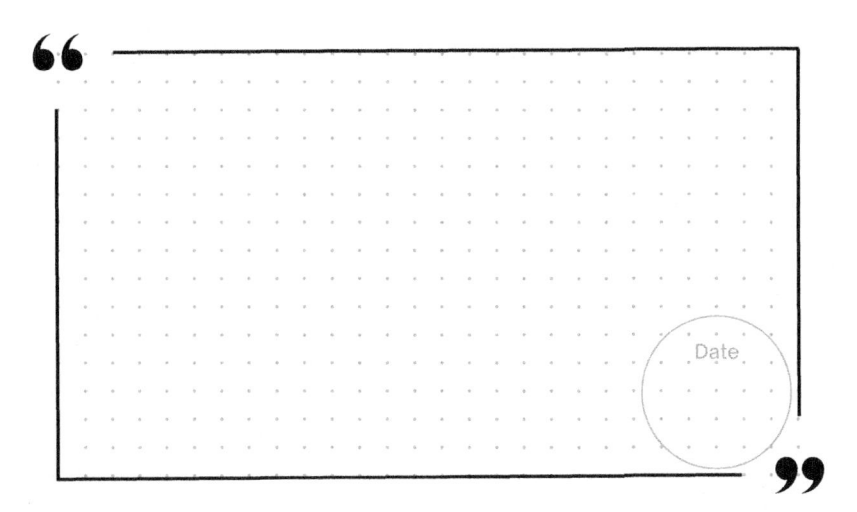

"

Date

"

Chapter 83

THERE'S NO SUCH THING AS NORMAL

- **Perceptions Vary:** What seems normal in one place or culture can be completely different elsewhere.
- **Personal Definition:** You have the power to define what is normal and right for your own life.
- **Challenge Norms:** Just because something is common doesn't mean it's ideal for you.

WHAT ASPECTS OF MY LIFE DO I CONSIDER 'NORMAL,' AND HOW CAN I REDEFINE THEM TO BETTER ALIGN WITH MY VALUES AND PREFERENCES?

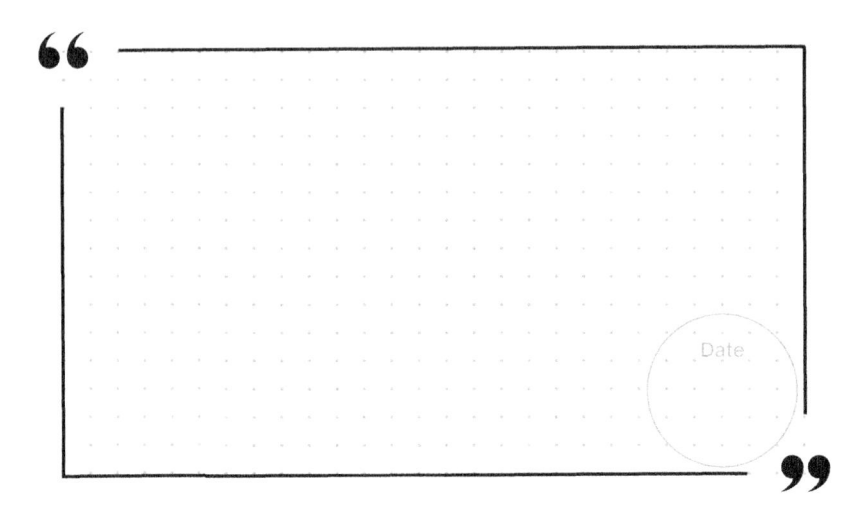

Date

Chapter 84

TAKE A STAND FOR THE "AND"

- **Embrace Dualities:** You can embody multiple roles and qualities at once, like being a parent and a CEO.
- **Challenge Limits:** The only limits are the ones you impose on yourself.
- **Expand Possibilities:** Adding more 'ands' to your life opens up new opportunities and experiences.

WHAT 'ANDS' DO I WANT TO ADD TO MY LIFE, AND HOW CAN I START PURSUING THEM?

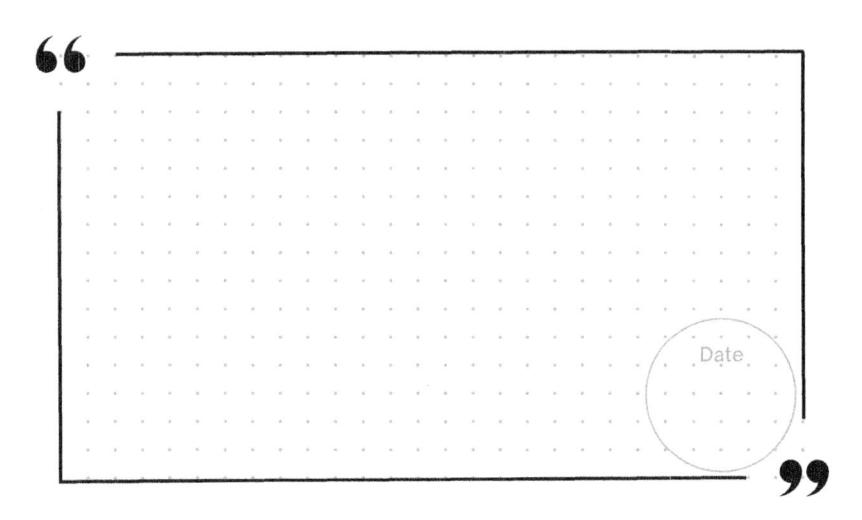

"

Date

"

Chapter 85

THE BIGGEST MANIFESTING MAGNETIZER: APPRECIATION

- **Reticular Activating System (RAS):** Your brain filters information, focusing on what matters to you.
- **Manifesting Through Focus:** What you appreciate and focus on becomes more visible in your life.
- **Appreciation Boosts Positivity:** By focusing on what's good, you attract more positive experiences and opportunities.

WHAT DO I ALREADY HAVE AND APPRECIATE THAT I WISH TO RECEIVE MORE OF?

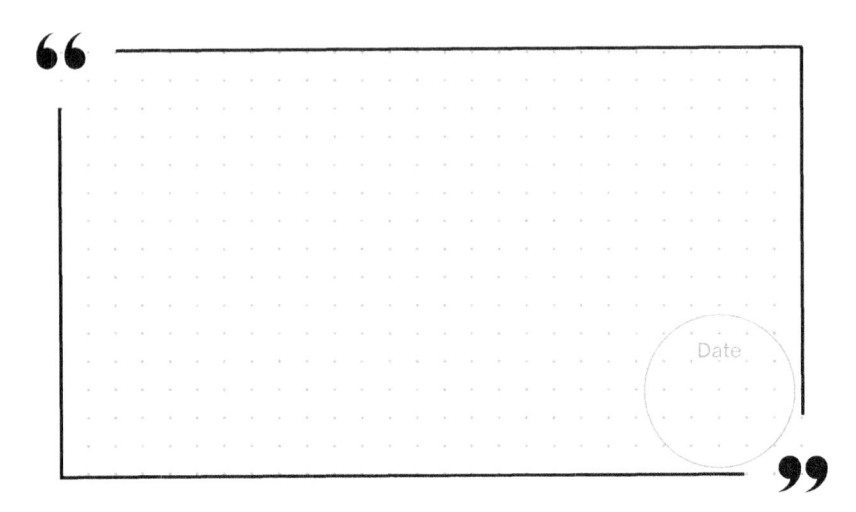

"

Date

"

Chapter 86

KEEP YOUR NETWORK ALIVE

- **Maintain Connections:** Regularly reach out to people you care about to keep relationships strong.
- **Simple Outreach:** Use brief messages or updates to stay in touch, even during busy moments.
- **Value Relationships:** The quality of life is enhanced by meaningful relationships, so make an effort to nurture them.

WHO ARE THE PEOPLE I WANT TO KEEP IN MY LIFE, AND HOW CAN I REACH OUT TO THEM MORE REGULARLY?

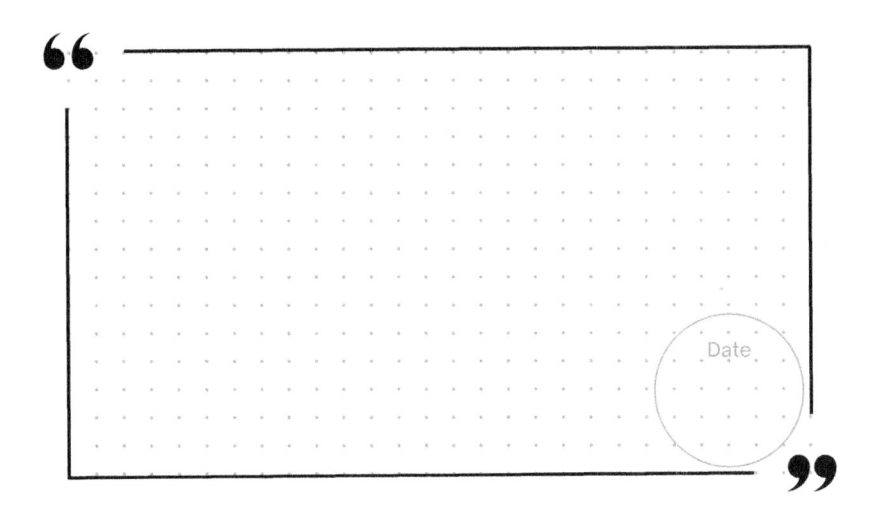

"

Date

"

Chapter 87

PITY IS NEVER HELPFUL

- **Avoid Pity:** Pity can make situations worse and is not supportive.
- **Focus on Strengths:** Recognize and affirm others' strengths and capabilities.
- **Empowerment:** Viewing others in their wholeness helps them see their true potential.

WHO IN MY LIFE COULD BENEFIT FROM SEEING THEIR STRENGTHS AND CAPABILITIES, AND HOW CAN I REMIND THEM OF THEIR TRUE WORTH?

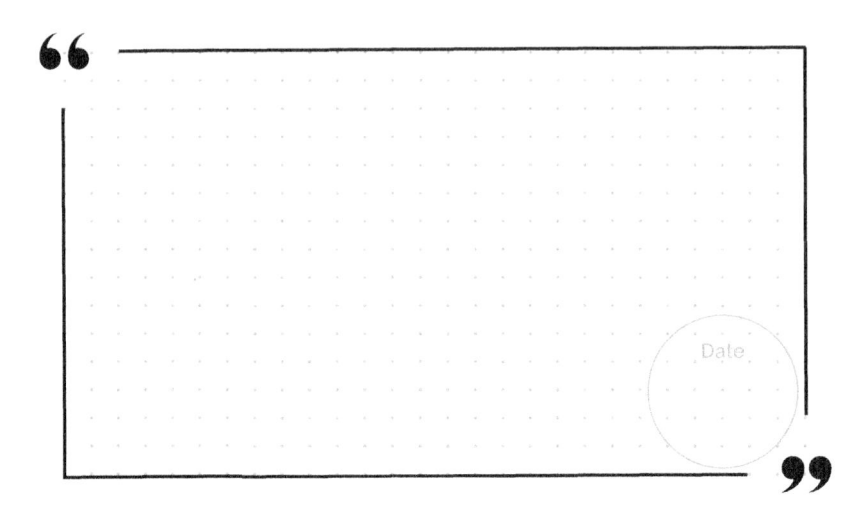

Date

Chapter 88

DIVORCE IS NOT A BIG DEAL

- **Divorce and Courage:** Divorce isn't life-ending; it's a result of having the courage to believe in something that didn't work out.
- **Acceptance:** It's okay if things don't go as planned; it's part of life's reality.
- **Perspective:** The universe values everyone equally, regardless of their marital status.

ARE THERE AREAS IN MY LIFE WHERE I NEED TO ACCEPT THAT THINGS DIDN'T TURN OUT AS PLANNED, AND HOW CAN I EMBRACE THE LESSONS LEARNED?

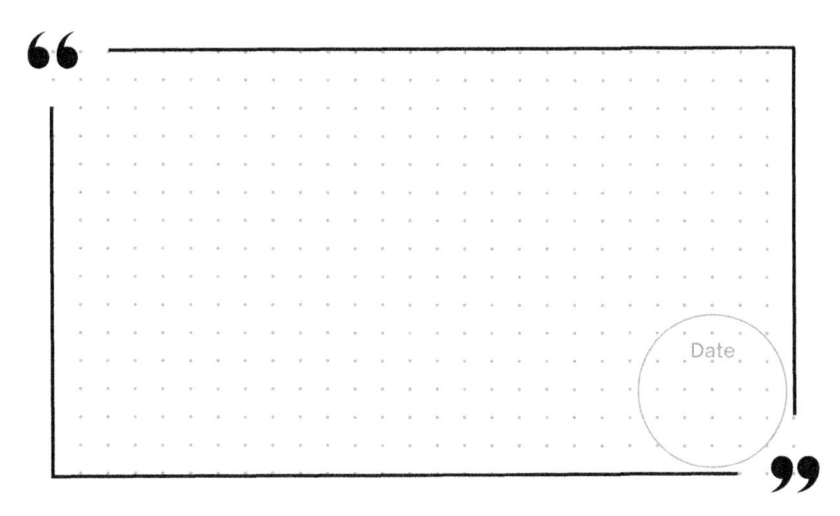

"

Date

"

Chapter 89

THE SECRET TO CONTENTMENT - EVEN IF YOU FEEL LONELY OR SAD OR LOST

- **Appreciate What You Have:** Embrace and love what you have, even if it differs from traditional celebrations or expectations.
- **Find Joy in Small Things:** Contentment comes from valuing everyday blessings and making the most of your current situation.
- **Gratitude Expands:** Focus on what you're thankful for to enhance your sense of abundance.

WHAT ASPECTS OF MY LIFE AM I TRULY GRATEFUL FOR, AND HOW CAN I SHIFT MY FOCUS TO APPRECIATE THESE MORE DEEPLY?

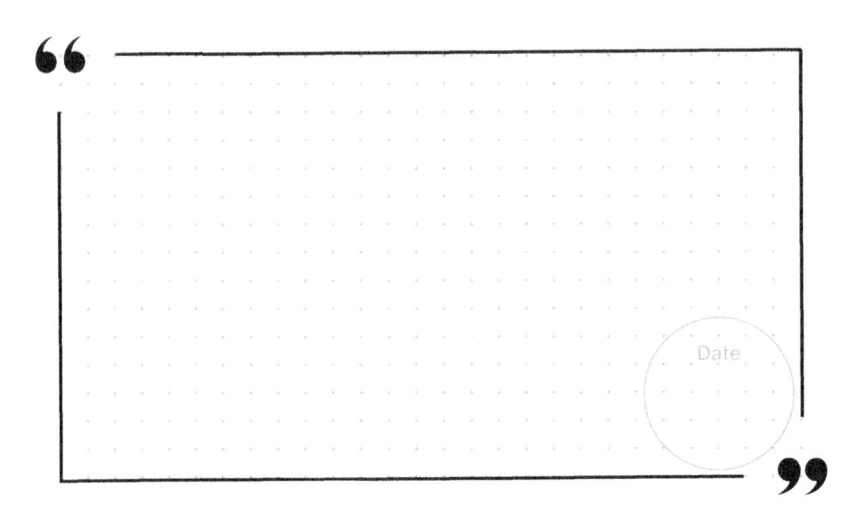

Date

Chapter 90

SULKING IS WORSE THAN FIGHTING

- **Conflict is Normal:** Fights in relationships are natural and not a sign of failure.
- **Bounce Back Quickly:** The key to lasting relationships is recovering from conflicts swiftly, not avoiding them.
- **Avoid Sulking:** Extended sulking can harm relationships more than the original argument.

HOW CAN I ADDRESS CONFLICTS MORE CONSTRUCTIVELY AND AVOID SULKING?

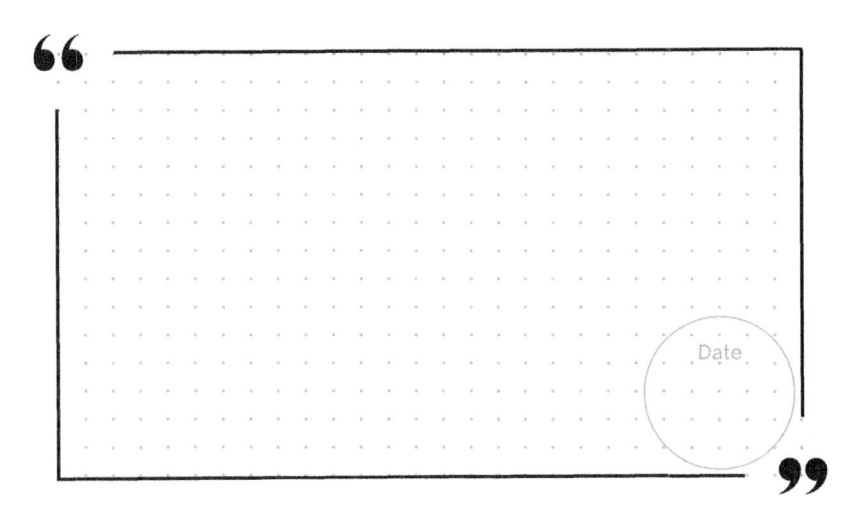

"

Date

"

Chapter 91

JUST 30 MINUTES IS ENOUGH

- **Short Time Blocks Can Be Productive:** You don't need long periods of uninterrupted time to be creative.
- **Use Pockets of Time:** Even 30 minutes can be highly effective for working on your goals.
- **Consistency Matters:** Small, consistent efforts accumulate over time.

WHAT SMALL, CONSISTENT ACTIONS CAN I TAKE IN JUST 30 MINUTES TO MOVE CLOSER TO MY CREATIVE GOALS?

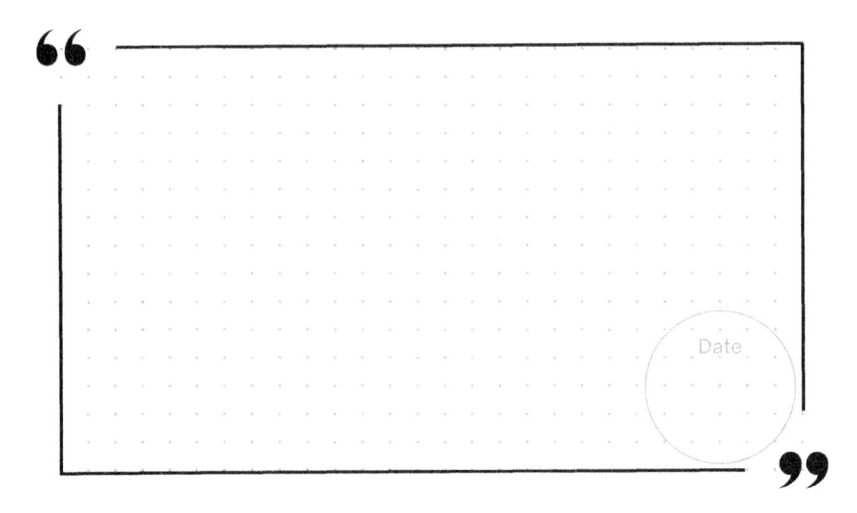

"

Date

"

Chapter 92

DON'T GIVE UP HOPE ON A STRAINED FAMILY RELATIONSHIP

- **Reconciliation is Possible:** Simple gestures, like reaching out, can mend strained family relationships and bring people closer.
- **Realistic Expectations:** Many families face dysfunction and challenges; the ideal of a perfect family is rare.
- **Value Relationships:** Even if family dynamics aren't ideal, it's important to appreciate and work on relationships when possible.

IS THERE A FAMILY RELATIONSHIP THAT I WISH TO HEAL? WHAT SMALL STEPS CAN I TAKE TO INITIATE OR CONTINUE THE PROCESS OF RECONCILIATION?

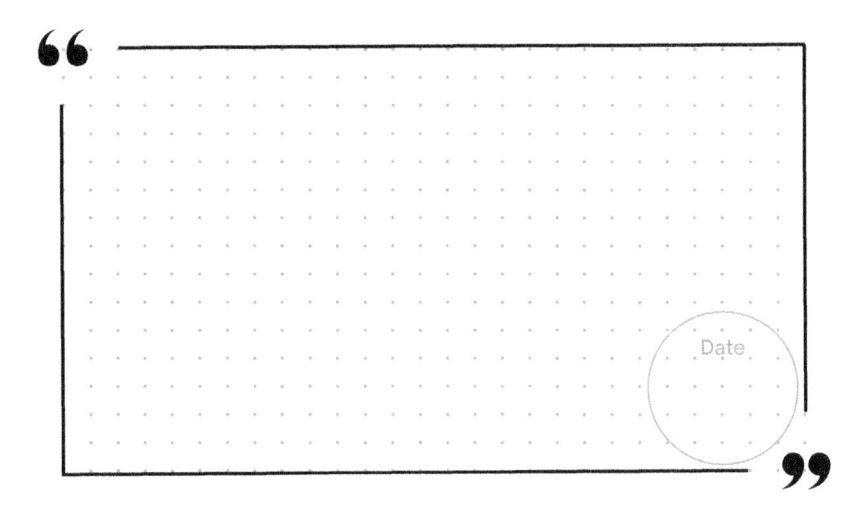

Date

Chapter 93

THE PICKUP LINE THAT RESULTED IN TWO HUSBANDS

- **Be Bold:** Taking the initiative to start a conversation can open up new relationships.
- **Embrace Discomfort:** Being willing to be a little uncomfortable can lead to valuable connections.
- **New Opportunities Await:** Stepping out and making the first move can lead to exciting and meaningful interactions.

WHO COULD I REACH OUT TO OR CONNECT WITH TODAY, AND HOW WILL I START THAT CONVERSATION?

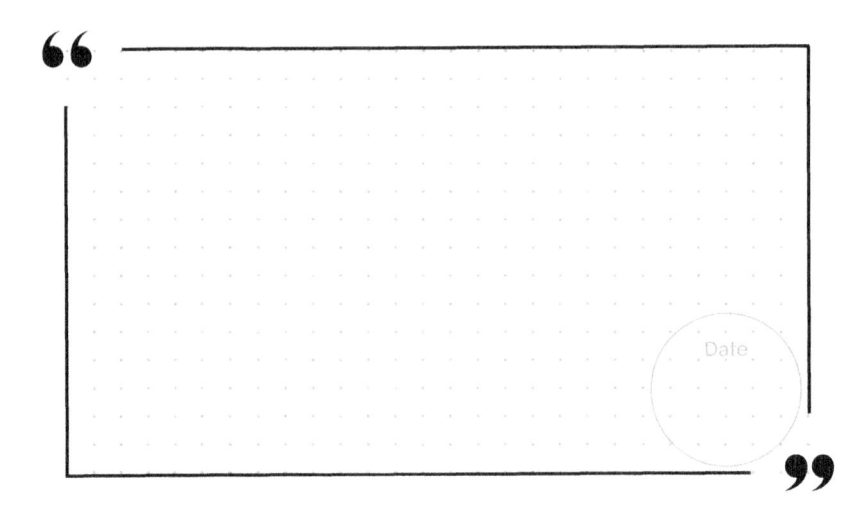

Date

Chapter 94

GIVE PEOPLE QUANTITY TIME

- **Quantity Time Matters:** While quality time is valuable, spending more time together can deepen relationships.
- **Real Connection Takes Time:** Meaningful relationships often develop through extended, everyday interactions rather than brief, intense moments.
- **Invest in Relationships:** Genuine connection comes from consistent, thoughtful presence over time.

WHO IN MY LIFE COULD BENEFIT FROM MORE OF MY TIME, AND HOW CAN I MAKE THAT HAPPEN?

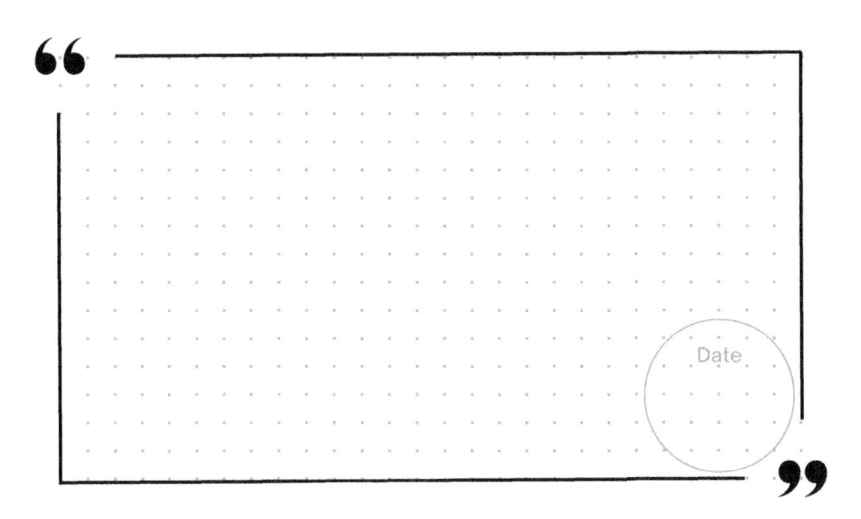

"

Date

"

Chapter 95

PRIORITY IS MEANT TO BE SINGULAR

- **Historical Context:** Originally, the term 'priority' was singular, reflecting the idea of having one main focus.
- **Modern Overload:** Today, we often list multiple priorities, which can dilute our focus and effectiveness.
- **Focus on One:** Distilling your priorities to just one per life area (work, health, family) can simplify and clarify your path.

WHAT IS MY ONE PRIORITY RIGHT NOW?

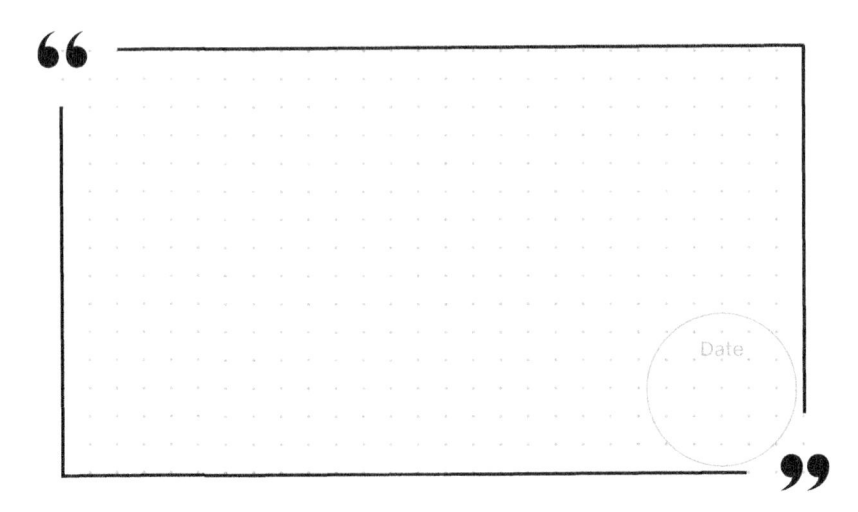

"

Date

"

Chapter 96

THE PURSUIT OF HAPPINESS IS MISERABLE

- **Accept All Emotions:** Happiness is one of many emotions; embrace the full range of feelings in life.
- **Focus on Moments:** Contentment comes from appreciating small, positive moments rather than seeking constant happiness.
- **Present Awareness:** Recognizing and valuing what's going well in the present enhances overall well-being.

HOW DO I DEFINE HAPPINESS?

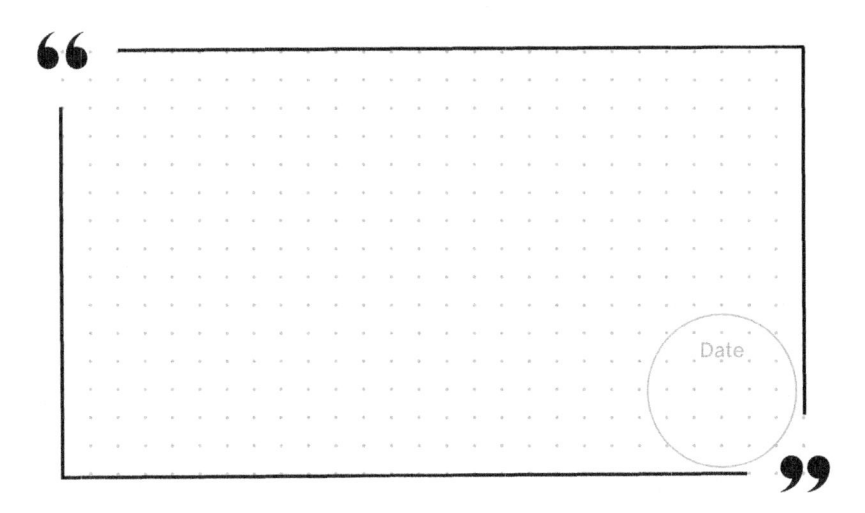

Chapter 97

DROP THE BALL SOMETIMES

- **Graceful Delays:** Delaying responses can let situations resolve on their own.
- **Manage Overwhelm:** Stepping back reduces stress and shows not everything needs immediate action.
- **Natural Resolution:** Many issues resolve without intervention.

WHAT TASKS OR RESPONSIBILITIES CAN I LET GO OF OR DELAY TO REDUCE MY STRESS?

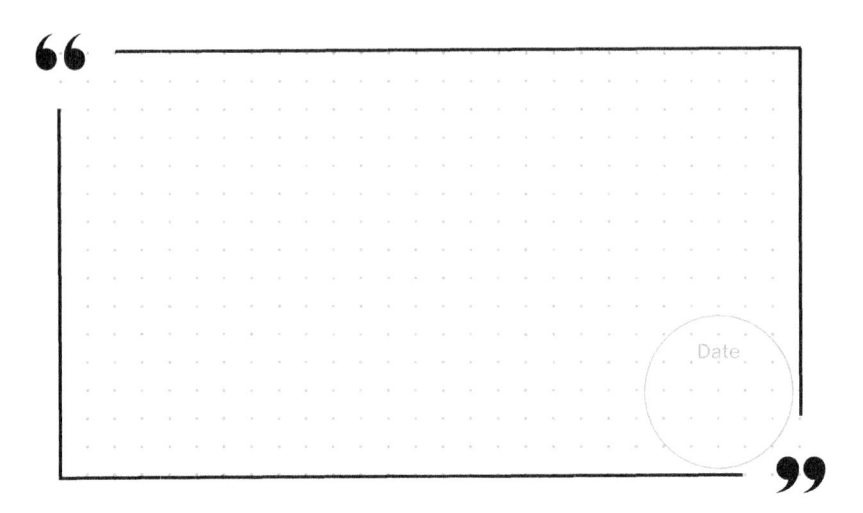

Chapter 98

IT'S BETTER TO BE HAPPY THAN RIGHT

- **Prioritize Peace:** Letting go of being right can bring more personal peace.
- **Avoid Resentment:** Holding onto anger can hinder progress and success.
- **Choose Happiness:** Happiness can be more valuable than correcting every wrong.

WHERE IN MY LIFE CAN I CHOOSE HAPPINESS OVER BEING RIGHT?

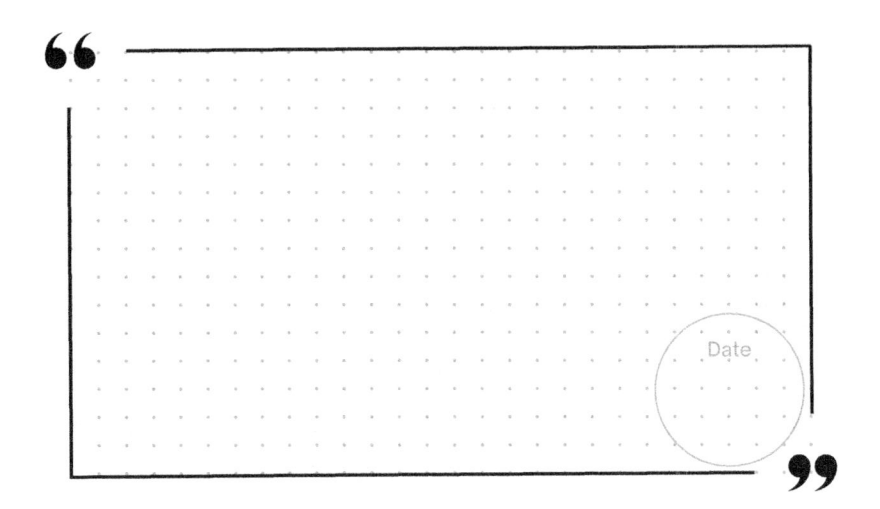

" "

Date

Chapter 99

ANTICIPATORY FEAR IS THE WORST KIND OF FEAR

- **Fear vs. Reality:** Anticipatory fear often exaggerates actual impacts.
- **Enjoy the Build-Up:** Anticipation can be as fulfilling as the event itself.
- **Reframe Your Fear:** Assess if your fear is justified and recognize its exaggerated nature.

IS MY CURRENT FEAR JUSTIFIED? HOW IS IT TRUE, AND HOW IS IT NOT TRUE? HOW DOES THE FEAR MAKE ME FEEL, AND CAN I LET IT GO KNOWING IT MIGHT BE WORSE IN MY MIND THAN IN REALITY?

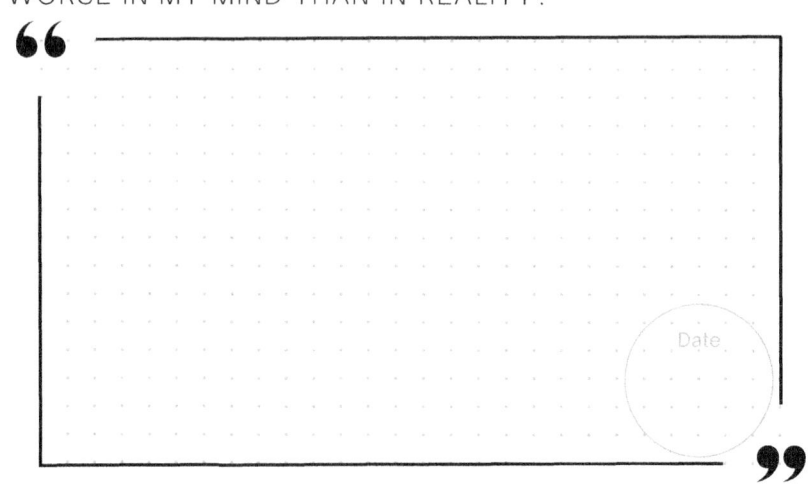

❝

Date

❞

Coping With My Fear

MY FEAR: _____

1 Is my fear justified?

2 In what way is my fear true?

3 In what ways is it not true?

4 How do I feel, when fear takes over?

5 How can I let it go?

Date

Coping With My Fear

MY FEAR: _____

1. Is my fear justified?

2. In what way is my fear true?

3. In what ways is it not true?

4. How do I feel, when fear takes over?

5. How can I let it go?

Date

Coping With My Fear

MY FEAR: _____

1. Is my fear justified?

2. In what way is my fear true?

3. In what ways is it not true?

4. How do I feel, when fear takes over?

5. How can I let it go?

Date

Chapter 100

PUTTING YOURSELF DOWN IS EXHAUSTING FOR OTHERS

- **Compliments as Gifts:** Rejecting compliments can drain those who give them.
- **Effort to Compliment:** Dismissing praise requires extra effort from others.
- **Gracious Acceptance:** Simply saying 'thank you' maintains positive interactions.

HOW CAN I ACCEPT COMPLIMENTS MORE GRACIOUSLY AND AVOID PUTTING MYSELF DOWN IN A WAY THAT MIGHT DISCOURAGE OTHERS?

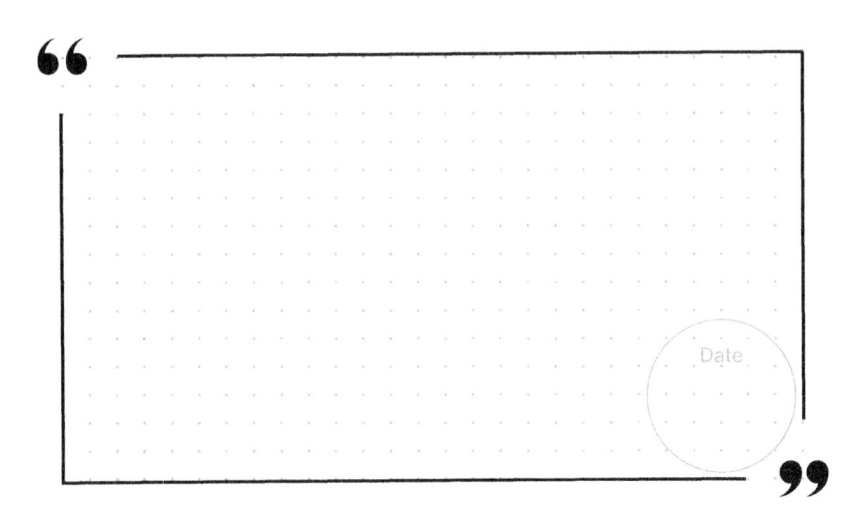

Date

Chapter 101

THE CORE OF ANY PHOBIA IS LOSS OF CONTROL

- **Fear of Losing Control:** Phobias often arise from a fear of losing control.
- **Focus on Control:** Identify and focus on what you can control to ground yourself.
- **Adapt Creatively:** Use your creativity to manage overwhelming situations.

WHAT IS MY BIGGEST PHOBIA, AND WHAT CAN I CONTROL IN SITUATIONS WHERE I FEEL FEAR?

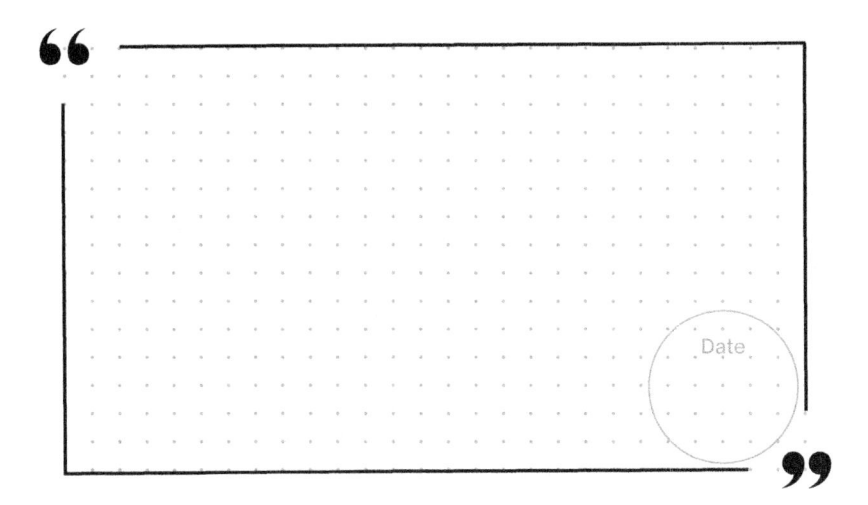

Date

Chapter 102

ACTIONS HAVE CONSEQUENCES

- **Consequences for All:** Actions, whether big or small, have consequences for everyone.
- **Reason Before Acting:** Use your ability to reason and think before making decisions to avoid regret.
- **Wisdom in Choices:** Recognize that wise choices consider the potential outcomes of your actions.

WHAT IS MY BIGGEST FEAR, AND WHAT CAN I CONTROL IN SITUATIONS WHERE I FEEL FEAR?

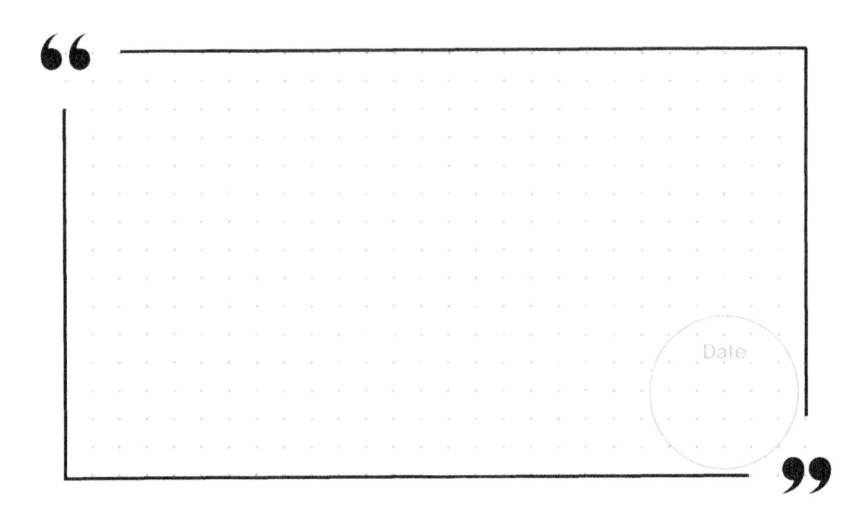

Date

Chapter 103

ASK YOURSELF, HOW MUCH OF MY LIFE WAS MY IDEA?

- **Reflect on Choices:** Assess how much of your life was shaped by your own decisions.
- **Empower to Change:** Remember you can choose and change aspects of your life.
- **Own Your Decisions:** Acknowledge your role in creating your current situation.

HOW MUCH OF MY CURRENT LIFE SITUATION WAS MY IDEA, AND WHAT CHANGES WOULD I MAKE IF I COULD CHOOSE AGAIN?

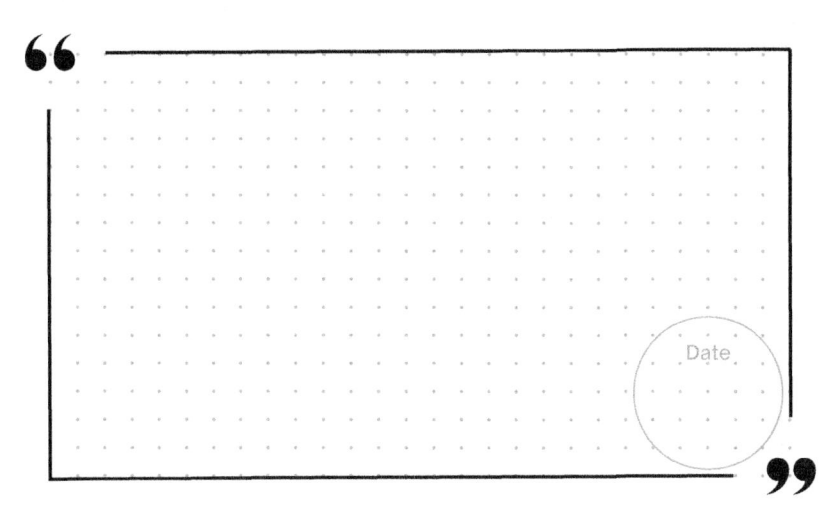

Date

Chapter 104

USE PERSPECTIVE TO RELAX

- **Cosmic Scale:** Viewing the universe's vastness can make your worries seem smaller.
- **Historical Context:** Recognizing our brief human existence in Earth's long history can reduce stress.
- **Temporary Nature:** Accepting life's impermanence helps to alleviate pressure and gain perspective.

HOW CAN I USE THE PERSPECTIVE OF THE VAST UNIVERSE OR HISTORICAL CONTEXT TO RELAX AND PUT MY CURRENT WORRIES INTO PERSPECTIVE?

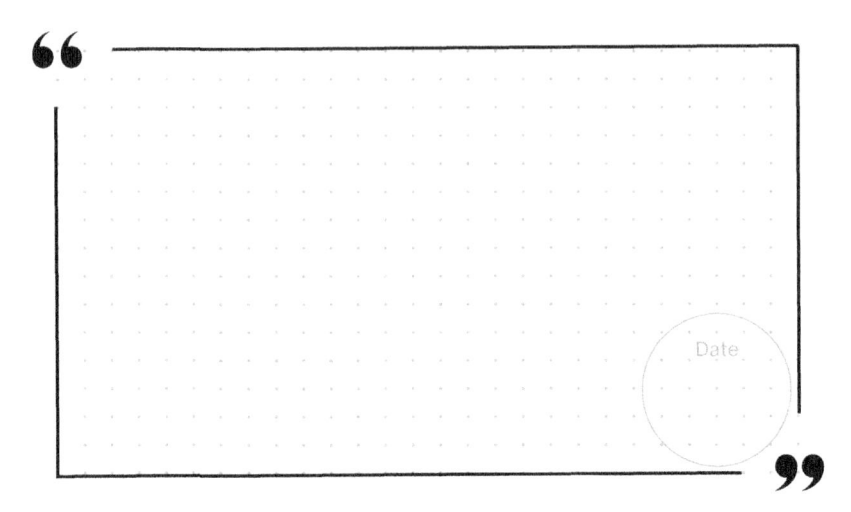

"

Date

"

Chapter 105

VICTIMS NEED VILLAINS

- **Blame Game:** Victims often seek villains to blame, creating unnecessary drama.
- **Distraction:** Drama can distract from more important tasks or goals.
- **Choice:** You have the power to decide how to respond and stay focused on your purpose.

WHO ARE THE VILLAINS IN MY WORLD, AND WHAT CAN I DO TO NOT LET THEM RUIN MY GOOD MOOD?

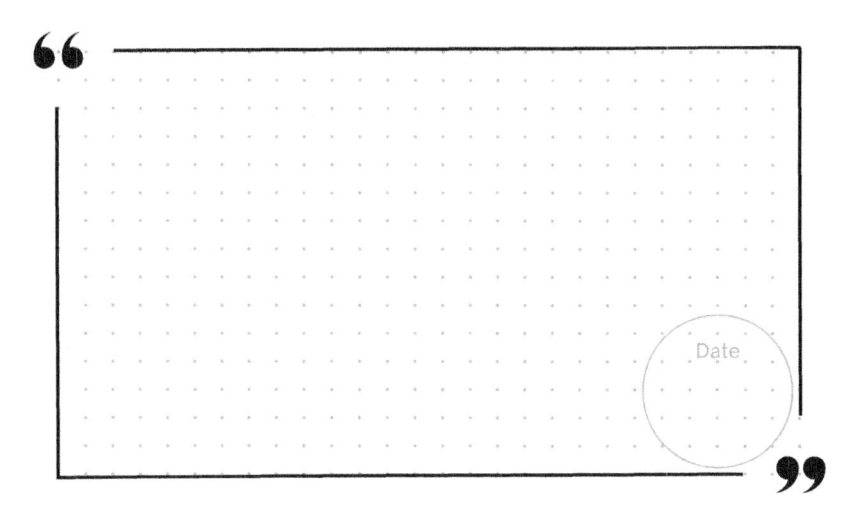

"

Date

"

Chapter 106

NEVER SAY, "I DON'T HAVE TIME"

- **Priority Truth:** Saying 'I don't have time' often means it's not a priority.
- **Honest Replacements:** Use specific statements like 'That's not a priority right now' or 'I need X time to complete it.'
- **Equal Time:** Everyone has 24 hours; it's about how you choose to spend them.

WHAT ARE MY TRUE PRIORITIES RIGHT NOW, AND HOW CAN I COMMUNICATE THEM MORE HONESTLY?

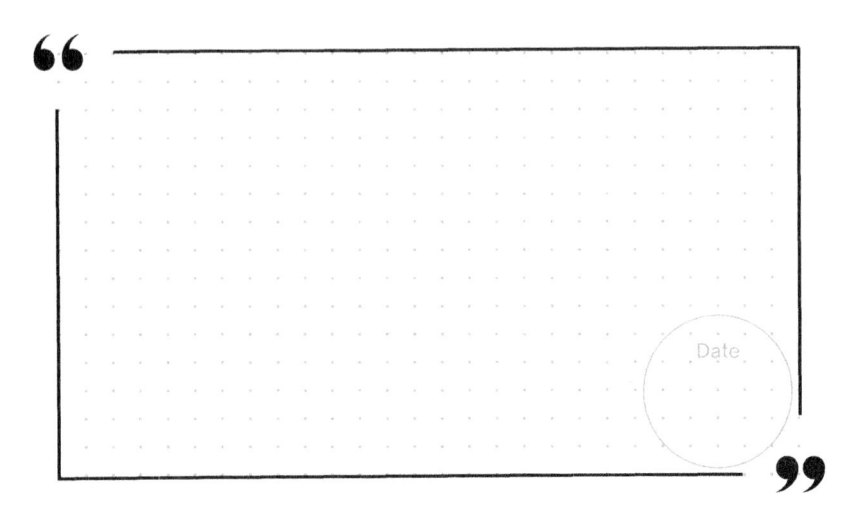

Date

Chapter 107

HUMANS ARE WIRED FOR MIMICRY

- **Mirror Neurons:** We mimic behaviors we observe due to mirror neurons.
- **Positive Reflection:** Act with enthusiasm and positivity to inspire the same response from others.
- **Influence Responses:** How you present yourself affects how others respond to you.

HOW CAN I USE MY BEHAVIOR TO POSITIVELY INFLUENCE HOW OTHERS RESPOND TO ME?

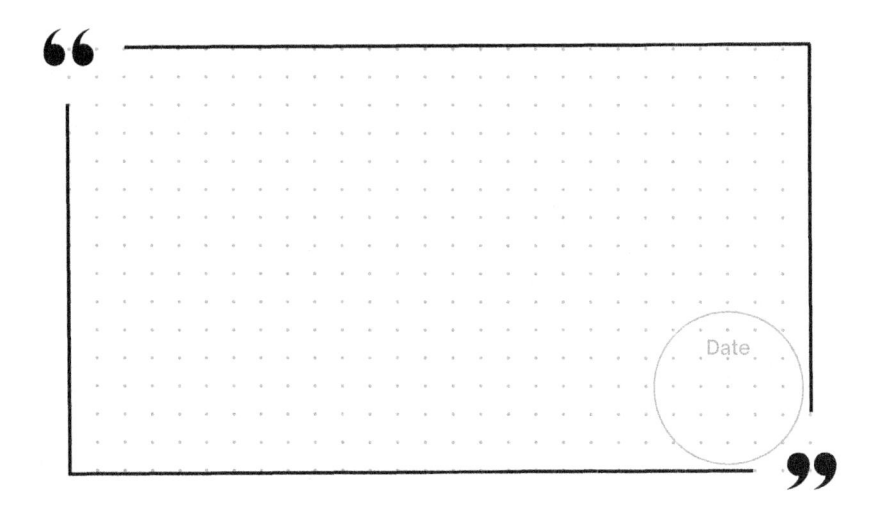

"

Date

"

Chapter 108

TAKE IT SERIOUSLY, BUT HOLD IT LIGHTLY

- **Balance Fun and Seriousness:** Combine enjoyment with professionalism for a more fulfilling experience.
- **Joy Boosts Creativity:** Embracing joy reduces stress and enhances creativity.
- **Add Fun to Your Day:** Infuse energy and fun into your routine to make work and life more enjoyable.

HOW CAN I ADD ENERGIZING FUN TO MY DAILY ROUTINE WHILE MAINTAINING A SERIOUS APPROACH TO MY GOALS?

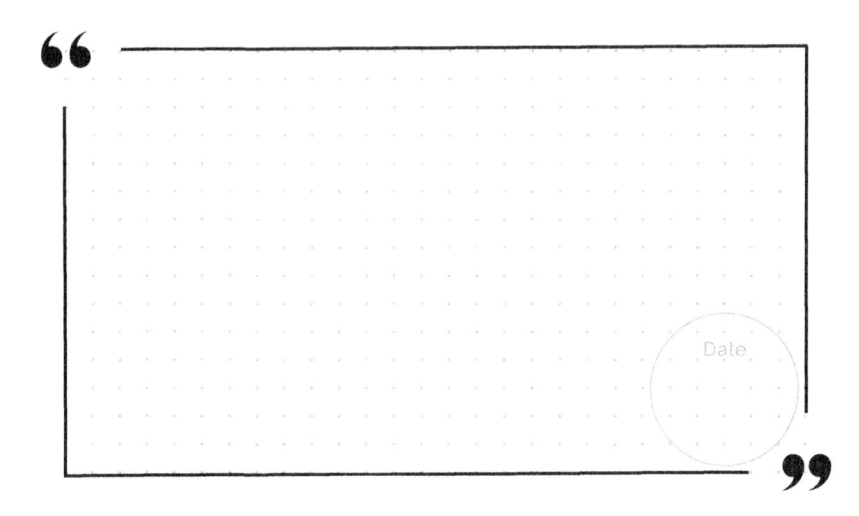

Date

Chapter 109

BE GENEROUS IN ORDER TO WIN

- **Generosity Attracts:** Giving more than expected often leads to greater rewards and positive responses.
- **Value Over Cost:** Generosity can be more impactful than strict pricing or minimal effort.
- **Long-Term Impact:** Offering extra value helps build lasting relationships and success.

HOW CAN I BE MORE GENEROUS IN MY ACTIONS OR INTERACTIONS TO CREATE POSITIVE OUTCOMES?

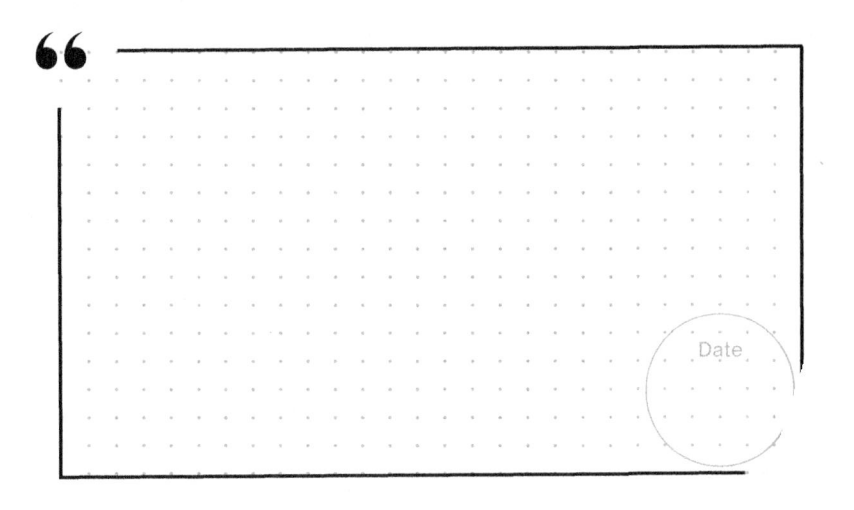

Date

Chapter 110

GIVE THE PEOPLE YOU LOVE PERMISSION TO DIE

- **Strength in Letting Go:** True strength can be found in allowing loved ones to leave without resisting their departure.
- **Acceptance of Death:** Acknowledging and accepting the inevitability of death can ease suffering and provide comfort.
- **Love Beyond Life:** Mourning and missing someone is a testament to the love shared and the impact they had on your life.

HOW CAN I SUPPORT LOVED ONES AND MYSELF BY ACCEPTING THE NATURAL COURSE OF LIFE AND DEATH?

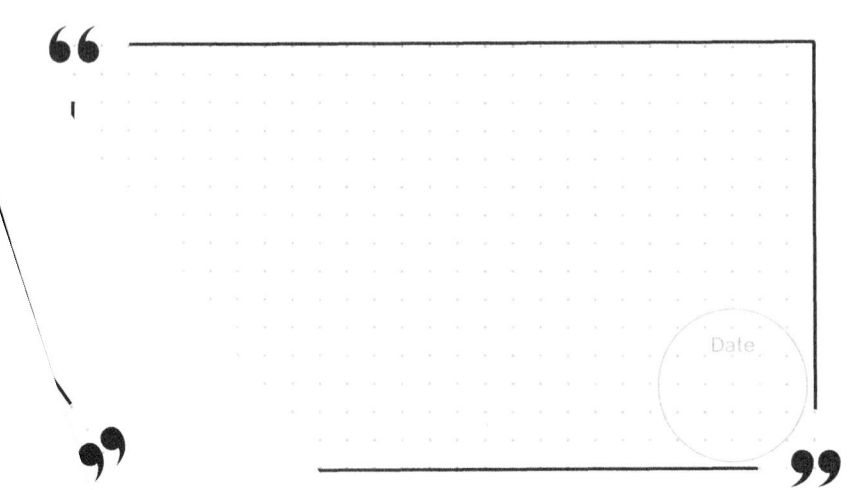

"
I

Date
"

Chapter 111

DESIRE REQUIRES DISTANCE SOMETIMES

- **Space Enhances Love:** Taking breaks and having personal space can reignite feelings of affection and appreciation.
- **Value Individuality:** Celebrating each other's achievements and interests can strengthen your connection.
- **Healthy Distance:** Even within a relationship, allowing room for individual growth and interests fosters a deeper bond.

HOW CAN I CREATE SPACE IN MY RELATIONSHIPS TO FOSTER A DEEPER SENSE OF APPRECIATION AND DESIRE?

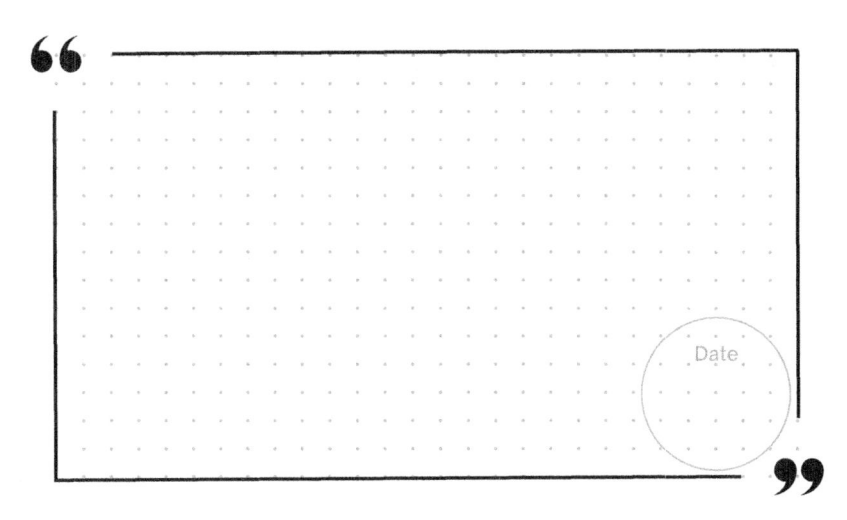

Date

Chapter 112

UNUSED TALENTS MAY AS WELL NOT EXIST

- **Value Action:** Talents need to be actively used to have value; otherwise, they may as well not exist.
- **Prioritize Goals:** Schedule time for important tasks and avoid distractions.
- **Act on Potential:** Regularly invest effort into your passions to realize their worth.

WHAT UNUSED TALENTS DO I HAVE THAT I NEED TO SHOW THE WORLD?

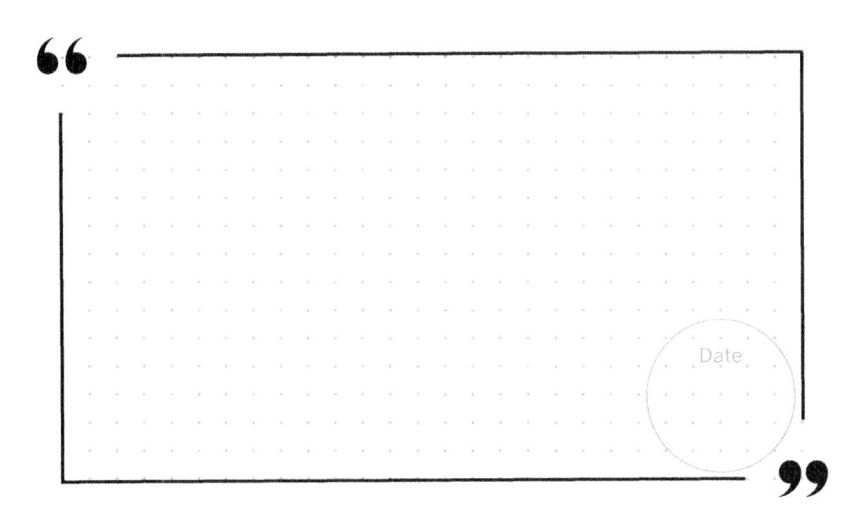

" "

Date

Chapter 113

HAPPINESS IS A SHORT MEMORY

- **Forget Negatives:** Let go of minor grievances and past slights to maintain happiness.
- **Focus Forward:** The happiest people move on from bad experiences quickly.
- **Selective Memory:** Choosing to forget unimportant issues can enhance well-being.

WHAT MINOR GRIEVANCES CAN I LET GO OF TO IMPROVE MY HAPPINESS?

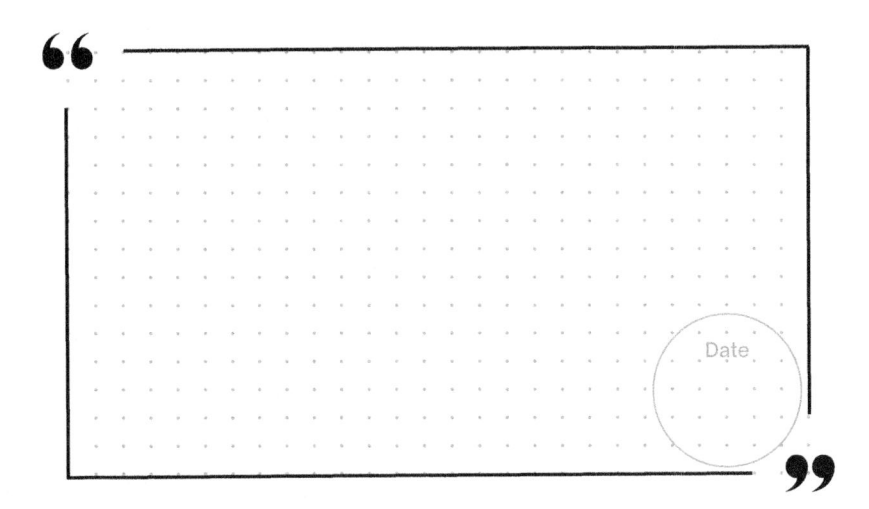

"

Date

"

Chapter 114

WHEN IN DOUBT, ZOOM OUT

- **Aerial View:** A broader perspective reveals true progress.

- **Avoid Panic:** Frequent checks can distort progress.

- **Patience:** Growth takes time; recognize it by zooming out.

WHERE AM I TODAY COMPARED WITH MY SITUATION ONE YEAR AGO?

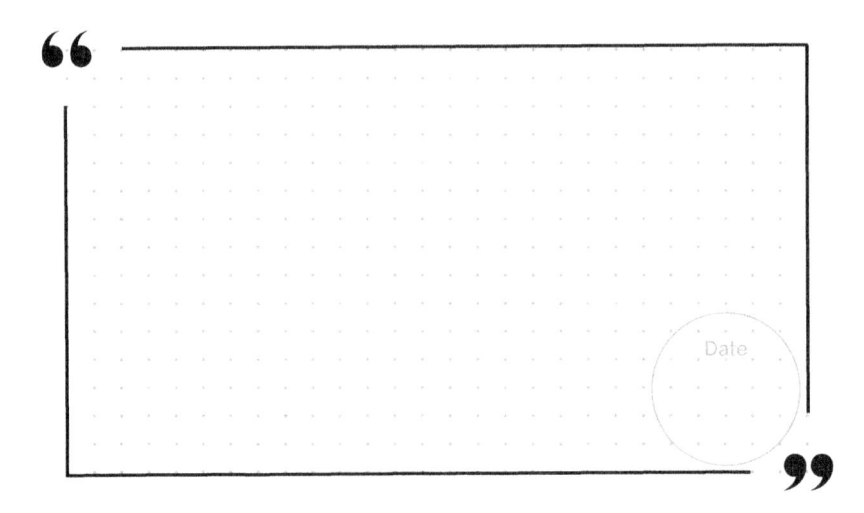

"
                                                                    Date
"

Chapter 115

DEFLATE DRAMA WITH DISTRACTION

- **Effective Distraction:** Shift focus to avoid escalating drama.
- **Positive Redirection:** Use conversation topics or events to diffuse tension.
- **Universal Technique:** Both kids and adults benefit from distraction to manage emotions.

HOW CAN I USE DISTRACTION TO DEFLATE DRAMA AND REDIRECT CONVERSATIONS EFFECTIVELY?

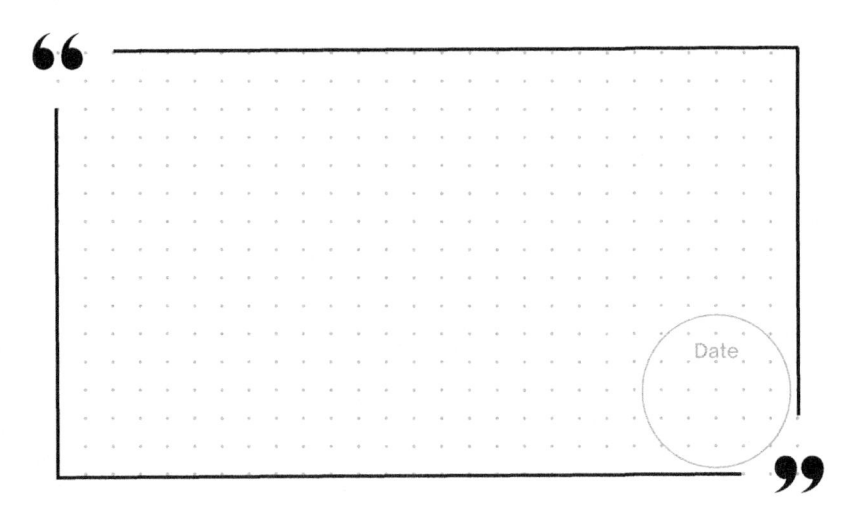

"
Date
"

Chapter 116

SAY SORRY FIRST

- **Initiate Reconciliation:** Be the first to apologize to mend important relationships.
- **Humility and Strength:** Apologizing requires both humility and courage.
- **Value Over Pride:** Prioritize the relationship over being right.

WHO DO I NEED TO APOLOGIZE TO, AND HOW CAN I MAKE THE FIRST MOVE TO MEND THAT RELATIONSHIP?

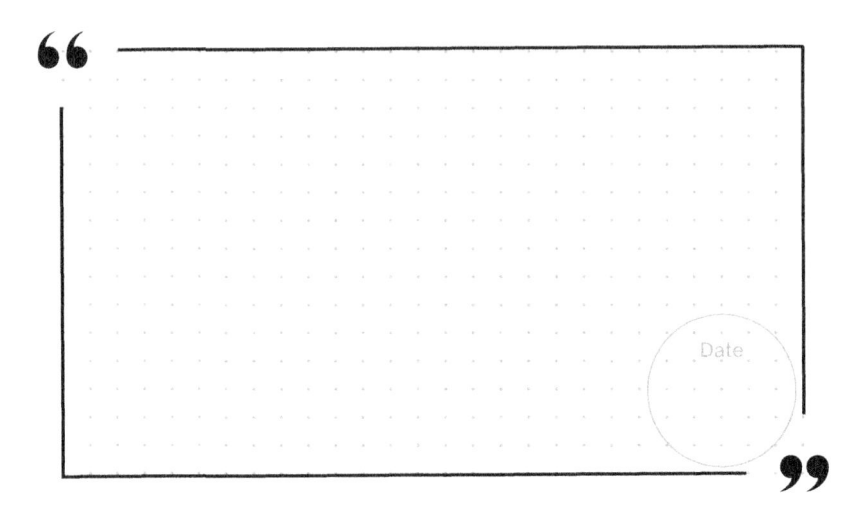

Chapter 117

BUILD TRUST WITH YOURSELF

- **Follow Through:** Trust yourself by keeping promises and following through on intentions.
- **Actions Build Trust:** Consistent actions, big or small, help establish self-trust.
- **Self-Worth:** You deserve to build trust with yourself through responsible actions.

HOW CAN I START FOLLOWING THROUGH ON MY INTENTIONS TODAY TO BUILD TRUST WITH MYSELF?

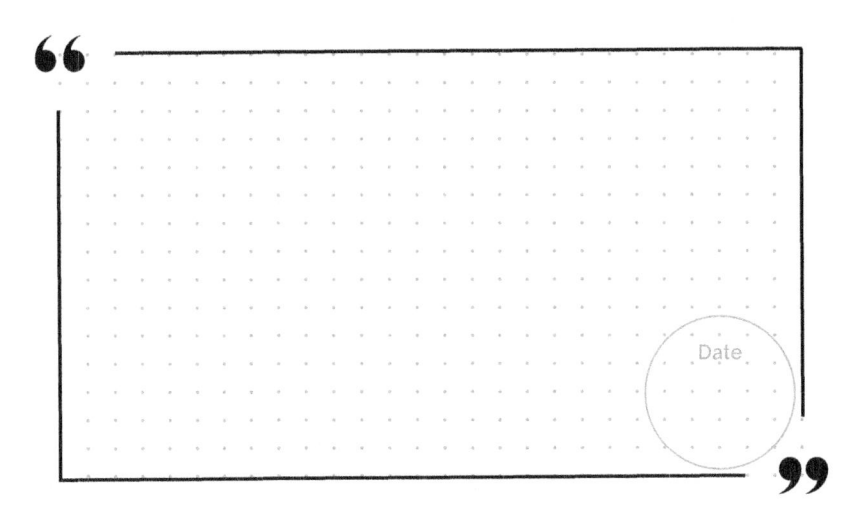

"

Date

"

Chapter 118

PEOPLE WHO DON'T TRUST CAN'T BE TRUSTED

- **Trust Reflection:** Distrust in others often reflects a lack of self-trust or trustworthiness.
- **Worldview:** Those who cannot trust are likely to see the world as deceitful and dangerous.
- **Choose Trust:** Being trusting and gullible can be preferable to a life filled with suspicion.

HOW DOES MY LEVEL OF TRUST IN OTHERS REFLECT MY OWN TRUSTWORTHINESS?

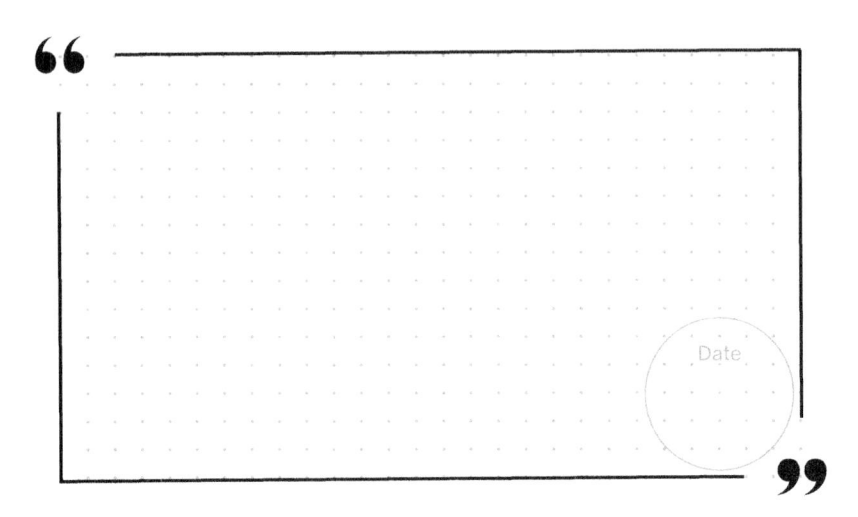

"

Date

"

Chapter 119

KNOW YOUR ONE THING

- **Identify Simplicity:** Find one small change that can significantly ease your life.
- **Examples:** Consistent routines, quitting habits, organizing, or new projects.
- **Ease Through Action:** Success and ease often come from simple, focused actions.

WHAT IS ONE SIMPLE CHANGE I CAN MAKE TO EASE MY LIFE?

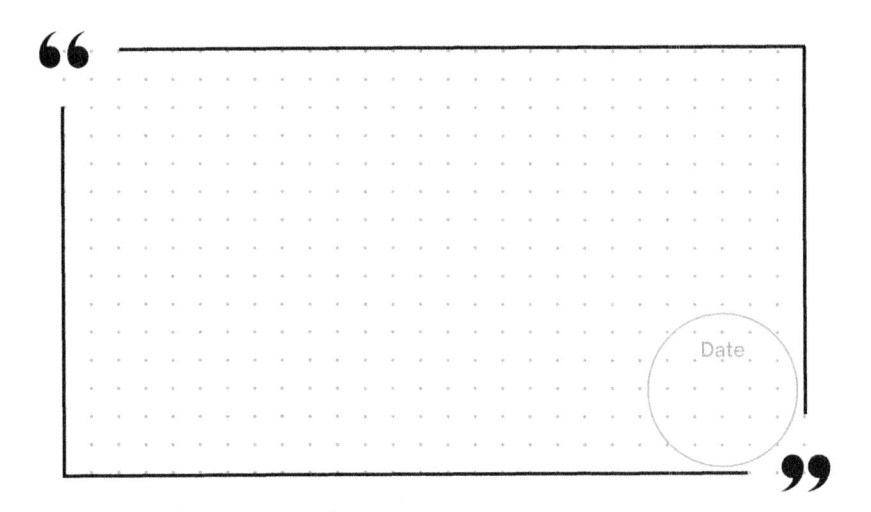

"

Date

"

Chapter 120

SEE THE CHILD IN EVERYONE

- **Imagine Youth:** Visualize others as children to build empathy and forgiveness.
- **Forgiveness Exercise:** By seeing their innocence, you can better understand and forgive them.
- **Self-Compassion:** Treat yourself with the same kindness and patience you would a child.

WHO DO I NEED TO SEE AS A CHILD RIGHT NOW TO HELP ME FORGIVE THEM AND UNDERSTAND THEM BETTER?

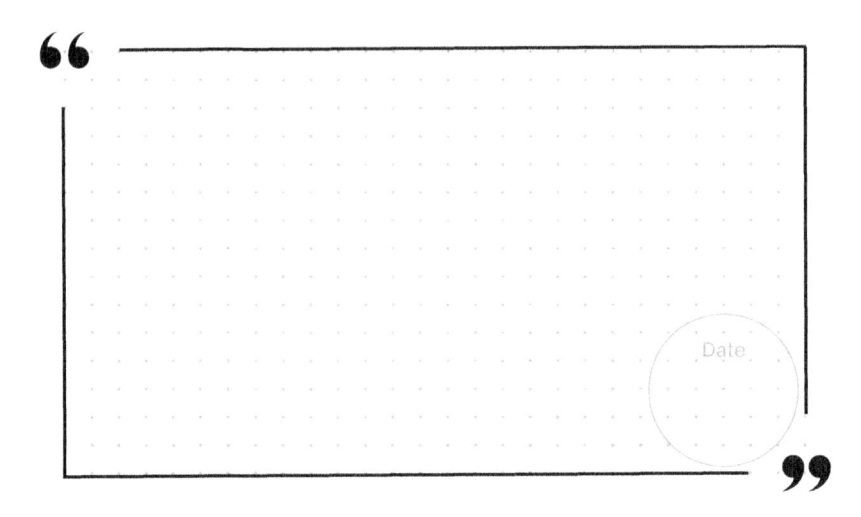

"

Date

"

Chapter 121

LOVE IS WHAT MAKES A FAMILY

- **Family Beyond Blood:** True family is defined by love, not just by biological connections or traditional setups.
- **Cherished Moments:** Personal experiences, like watching TV shows with loved ones or making friends at summer camp, can form deep bonds.
- **Broader Definition:** Family can be made up of friends, neighbors, or anyone who provides love and support, transcending conventional definitions.

WHO IN MY LIFE, BEYOND MY BIOLOGICAL FAMILY, REPRESENTS THE LOVE AND SUPPORT THAT MAKE UP MY TRUE FAMILY?

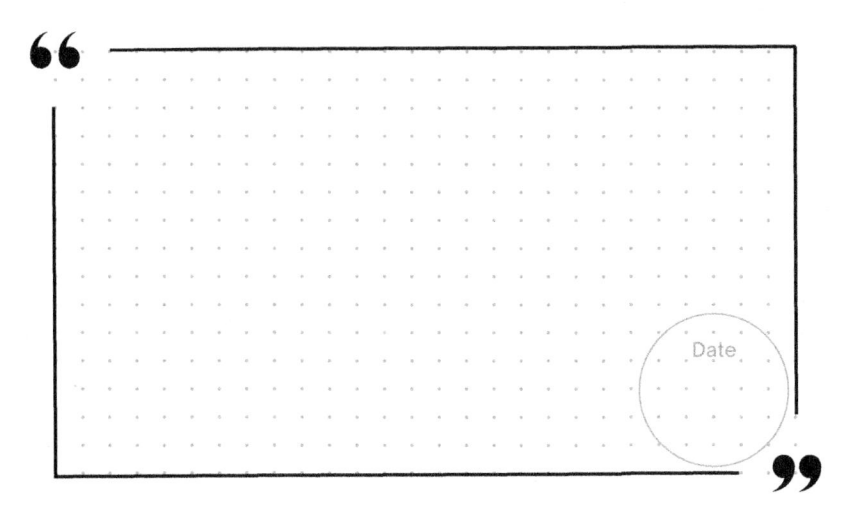

Date

Chapter 122

FOUR WORDS TO BE WARY OF USING

- **Words to Avoid:** Be cautious of using absolute words like 'always,' 'never,' 'everybody,' and 'nobody.'
- **Impact on Communication:** These words can escalate conflicts or self-doubt by exaggerating situations and creating unrealistic expectations.
- **Focus on Truth:** Using more precise and truthful language helps in clearer communication and reducing unnecessary negativity.

WHEN WAS THE LAST TIME I USED WORDS LIKE 'ALWAYS' OR 'NEVER' IN A CONVERSATION OR SELF-TALK? HOW CAN I REFRAME MY LANGUAGE TO BE MORE ACCURATE AND CONSTRUCTIVE?

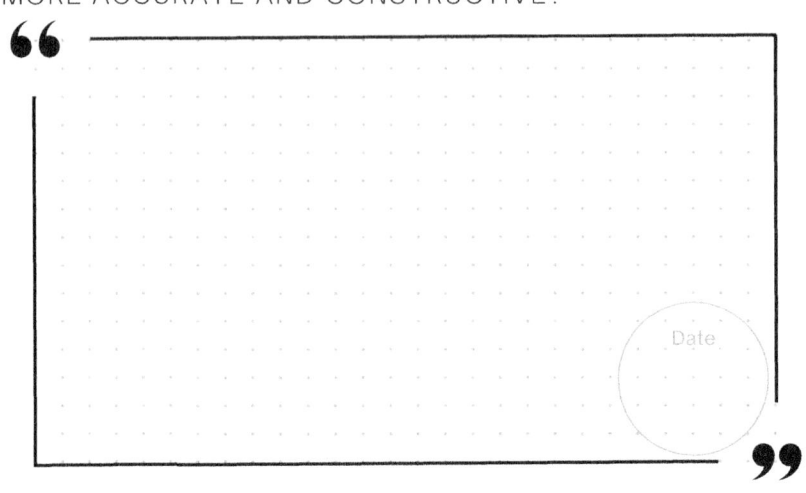

Date

Chapter 123

WHEN YOU WANT TO GIVE UP, REMEMBER THIS

- **Tribe's Secret:** An African tribe makes it rain through persistent dancing.
- **Persistence Wins:** Their success comes from never giving up.
- **Personal Challenge:** Apply the same principle of persistence to your own obstacles.

WHAT IS A CHALLENGE I'M FACING WHERE I FEEL LIKE GIVING UP? HOW CAN I APPLY THE PRINCIPLE OF PERSISTENCE TO KEEP GOING UNTIL I ACHIEVE MY GOAL?

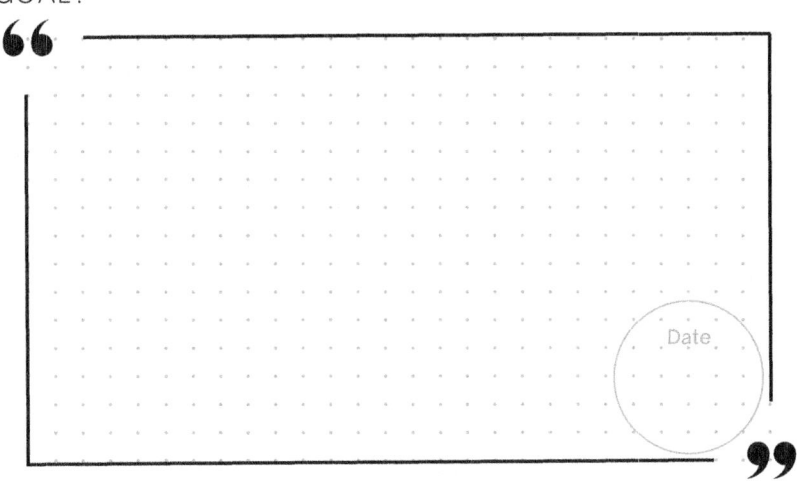

Date

Chapter 124

LIVE AND LET LIVE: THE ULTIMATE WISDOM

- **Letting It Be:** Sometimes the best choice is to avoid correcting others and enjoy the moment.
- **Focus on Yourself:** Happy people are less judgmental and more focused on their own lives.
- **Self-Care:** Avoiding unnecessary conflicts and judgments can be a powerful act of self-care.

WHERE CAN I PRACTICE LETTING THINGS BE INSTEAD OF CORRECTING OR JUDGING OTHERS?

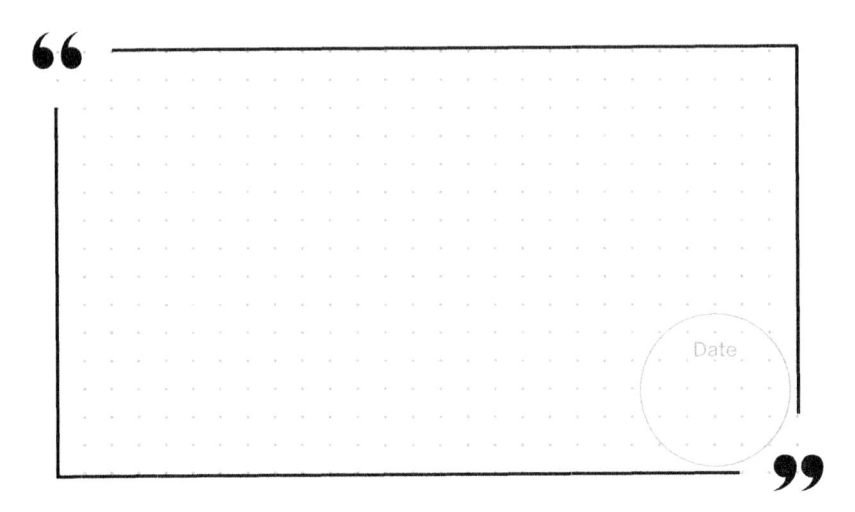

Date

Chapter 125

NOSTALGIA IS DANGEROUS

- **Distorted Memories:** Nostalgia can make past times seem better than they were.
- **Future Regret:** Current challenges may become future fond memories.
- **Enjoy Now:** The present can be the 'good old days' if we appreciate it.

WHAT AM I MISSING IN MY PRESENT BECAUSE I'M FOCUSED ON THE PAST?

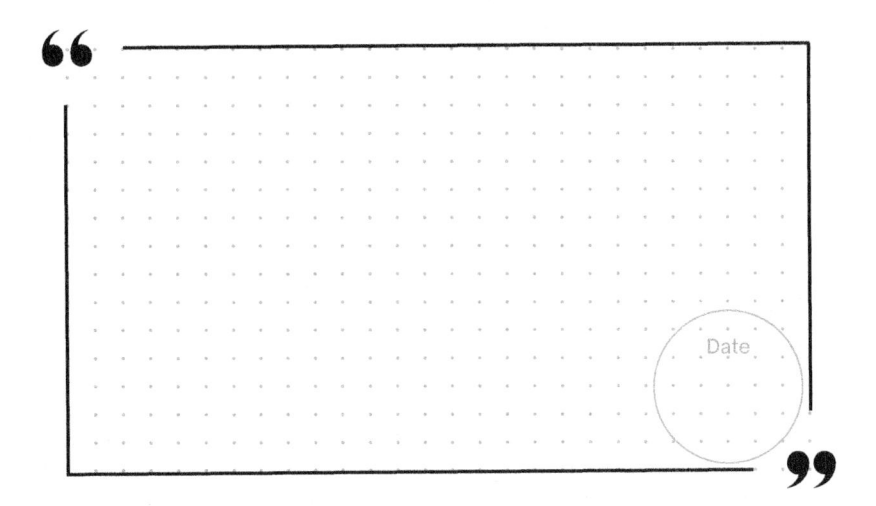

Date

Chapter 126

TOO LATE IS A DECISION, NOT A POSITION

- **No Expiration Date**: People don't have a set expiration date.
- **Late Starters**: Many achieve great things later in life.
- **Experience Advantage**: Experience is a strength, not a hindrance.

IS THERE SOMETHING I AVOID BECAUSE I THINK IT'S TOO LATE? HOW CAN I CHANGE THAT?

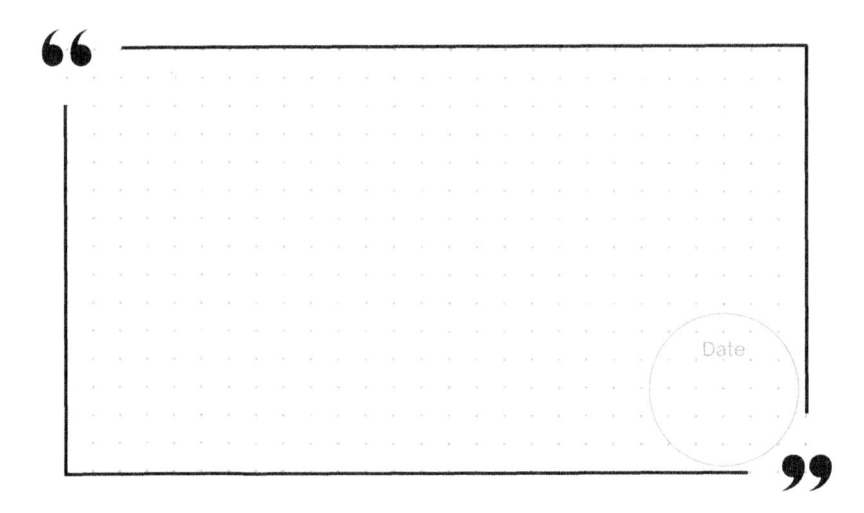

Date

Chapter 127

RAISE YOUR HAND EVEN WHEN YOU DON'T KNOW THE ANSWER

- **Embrace Uncertainty:** Trying, even without certainty, can lead to opportunities.
- **Act First:** Like buzzing in a game show, taking action may lead to unexpected answers.
- **Risk is Key:** Avoiding risks means missing out; courage involves stepping up and trying.

WHAT OPPORTUNITIES AM I AVOIDING BECAUSE I FEAR I DON'T HAVE ALL THE ANSWERS? HOW CAN I START TAKING ACTION?

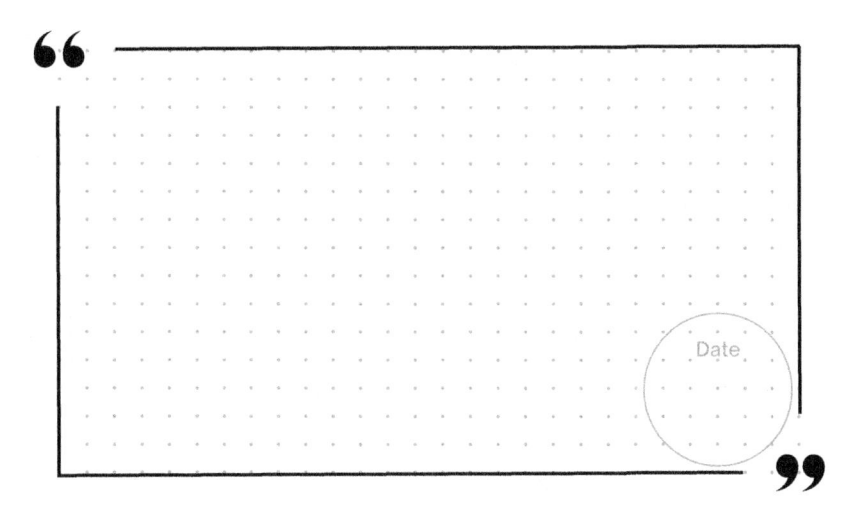

Date

Chapter 128

THERE'S NOTHING UNCOOL ABOUT PRACTICE

- **Value of Practice:** Skills need consistent practice to improve.
- **Behind the Scenes:** Success involves unseen effort and dedication.
- **Keep at It:** Perseverance through practice leads to progress.

WHAT WOULD I LIKE TO BE BETTER AT? WHAT DO I WISH TO PRACTICE MORE?

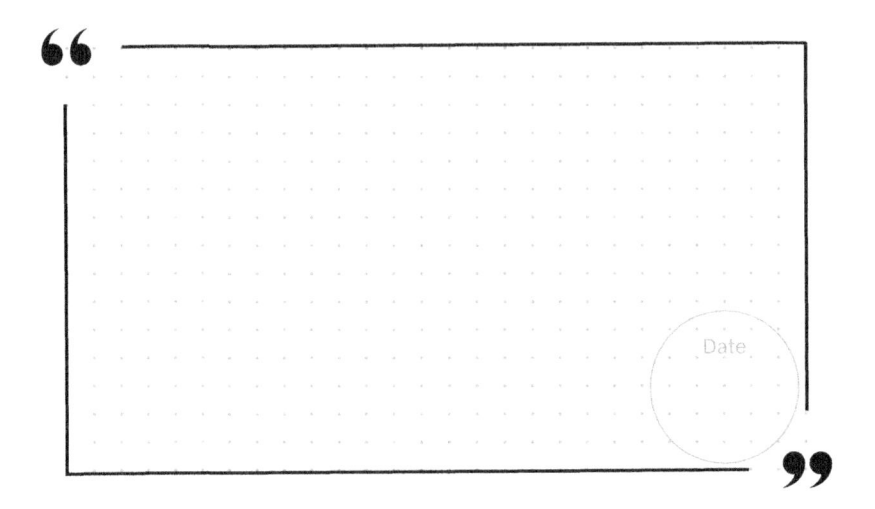

" "

Date

Chapter 129

FIND COMMONALITIES WITH YOUR "ENEMIES"

- **Look for Common Ground:** Disagreements often overshadow shared interests.
- **Value Differences:** Finding commonalities can lead to unexpected connections and learning.
- **Open Mind:** Approach conflicts with curiosity and openness rather than judgment.

WHO IS SOMEONE I DISAGREE WITH? WHAT COMMONALITIES CAN I FIND WITH THEM?

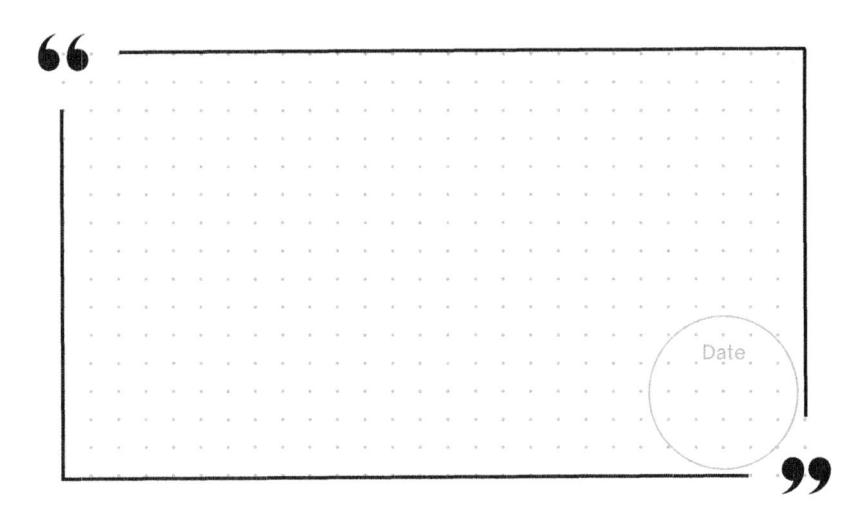

Chapter 130

LET SELLING BE EASY

- **Selling as Value Exchange:** Simplify the concept of selling to an exchange of value, which can make the process less intimidating.
- **Persuasion vs. Force:** Use persuasion rather than force to achieve your goals, both in sales and personal interactions.
- **Prepare and Persist:** Preparation builds confidence, and persistence drives success.

WHAT DO I WISH TO PERSUADE SOMEONE TO DO OR BUY RIGHT NOW?

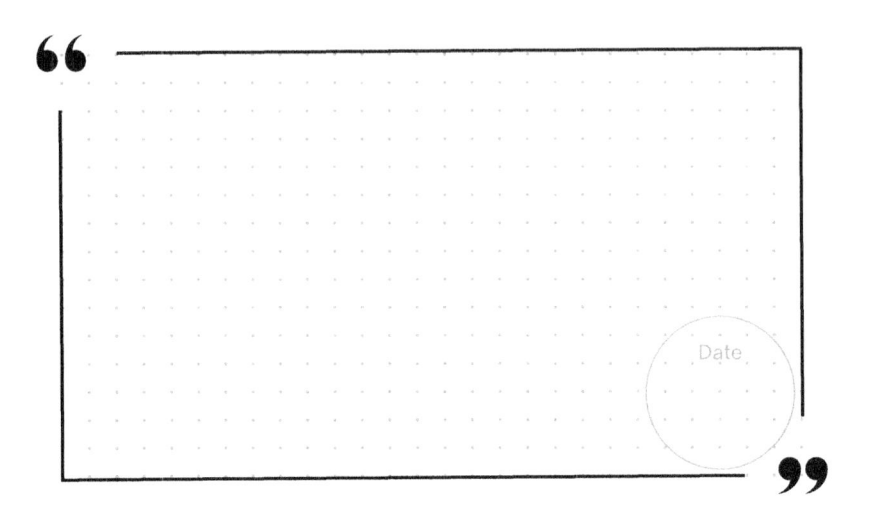

"

Date

"

How To Sell

PURPOSE: WHAT DO I WANT TO ACHIEVE?

Date

PREPARE: WHY DO I WANT THIS?

Date

How To Sell

> **PRESENT:** HOW TO SHARE THIS WITH PRESENCE?
>
> *Date*

> **PRESEVERE:** HOW I FOLLOW UP WITH PATIENCE
>
> *Date*

Chapter 131

BE FLEXIBLE WHEN UNEXPECTED THINGS HAPPEN

- **Embrace Flexibility:** When plans go awry, staying flexible reduces stress and fosters creativity.
- **Focus on Solutions:** Shift focus from problems to possibilities to enhance productivity and calm.
- **Ease Affects Others:** Your flexibility can ease stress for those around you, leading to smoother outcomes.

HOW CAN I REMAIN FLEXIBLE WHEN MY PLANS CHANGE? WHAT STRATEGIES CAN I USE TO FOCUS ON SOLUTIONS INSTEAD OF PROBLEMS?

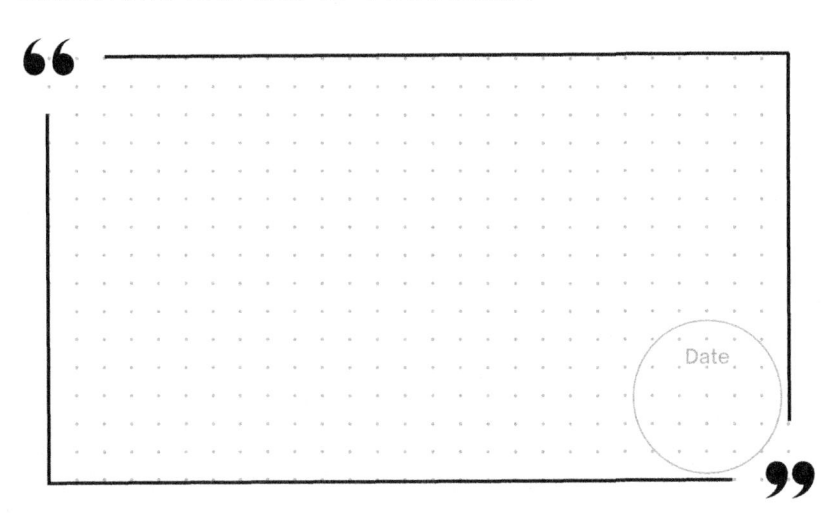

Date

Chapter 132

ONE DAY, YOU WON'T EVEN BE A FILE IN A HOSPITAL

- **Embrace the Temporary:** Life is fleeting, and records of our existence are temporary. Use your time wisely.
- **Create and Live Fully:** Don't let fear stop you from creating and living fully while you can.
- **Focus on the Present:** Take action now and focus on what brings you joy and fulfillment.

WHAT CAN I START DOING TODAY TO ENSURE I LIVE FULLY AND CREATE MEANING WHILE I STILL HAVE TIME?

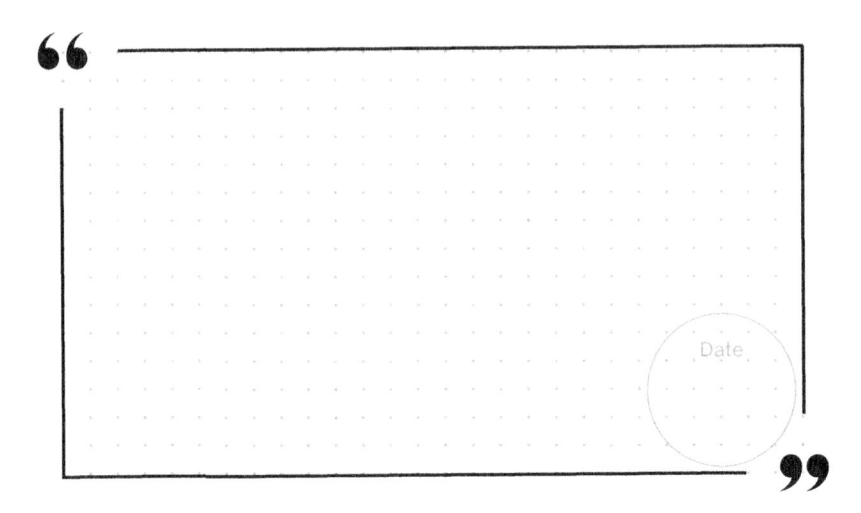

"

Date

"

Chapter 133

REPLACE YOUR KNIFE WITH AN AXE

- **Invest in Learning:** Sharpening your skills (like Abraham Lincoln sharpening his axe) saves time and effort in the long run.
- **Embrace the Learning Curve:** Initial difficulty in learning something new is often outweighed by the ease it brings later.
- **Continual Improvement:** Upgrading your skills keeps you sharp and adaptable.

WHAT SKILL CAN I START LEARNING TODAY THAT WILL MAKE MY LIFE EASIER?

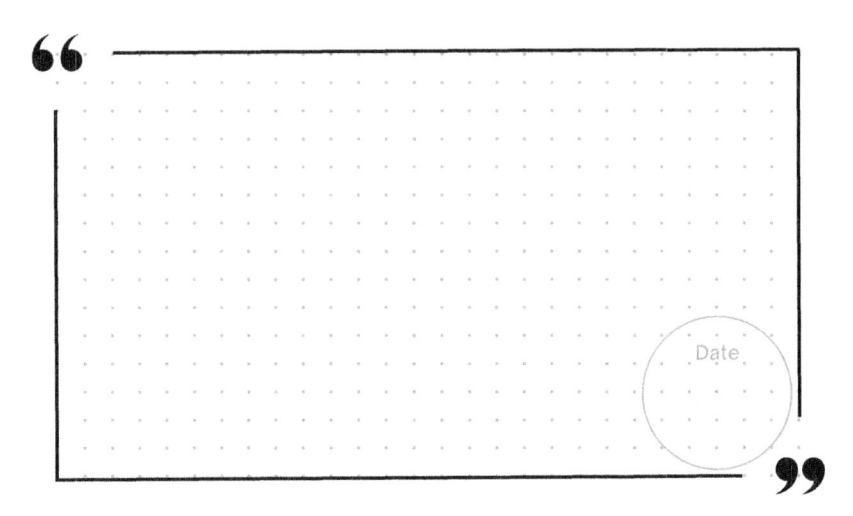

" "

Date

Chapter 134

BATCH YOUR LIFE!

- **Batch Tasks:** Group similar tasks together to improve efficiency and focus.
- **Minimize Distractions:** Avoid switching between tasks to reduce attention residue and enhance performance.
- **Streamline Processes:** Tackle tasks in focused bursts, like baking a batch of cookies, for faster completion.

WHAT TASKS CAN I BATCH TOGETHER TO STREAMLINE MY WORKFLOW AND BOOST MY PRODUCTIVITY?

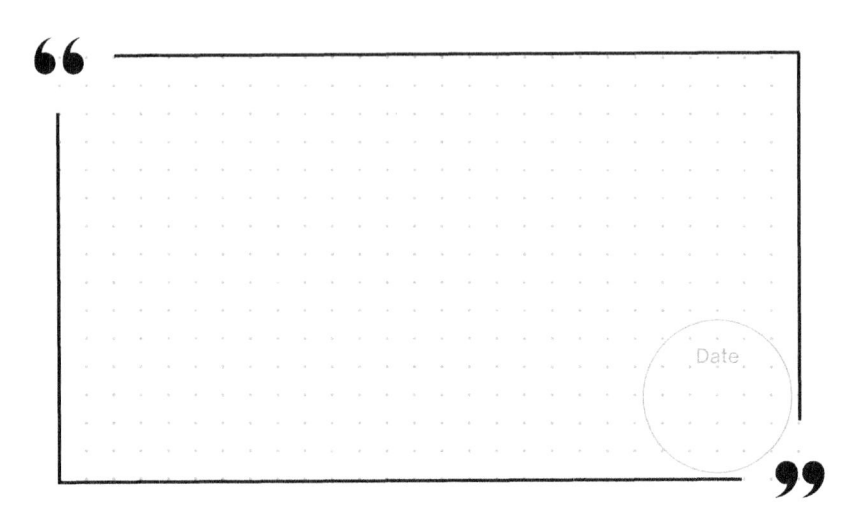

Date

Chapter 135

THE BEST WAY TO MAKE A FRIEND

- **Initiate Connection:** Reach out and make an effort to connect with others.
- **Show Up:** Be present and attentive in your friendships.
- **Give to Receive:** Offer what you wish to receive from others.

WHO WOULD I LIKE TO BEFRIEND, AND WHAT CAN I DO FOR THEM?

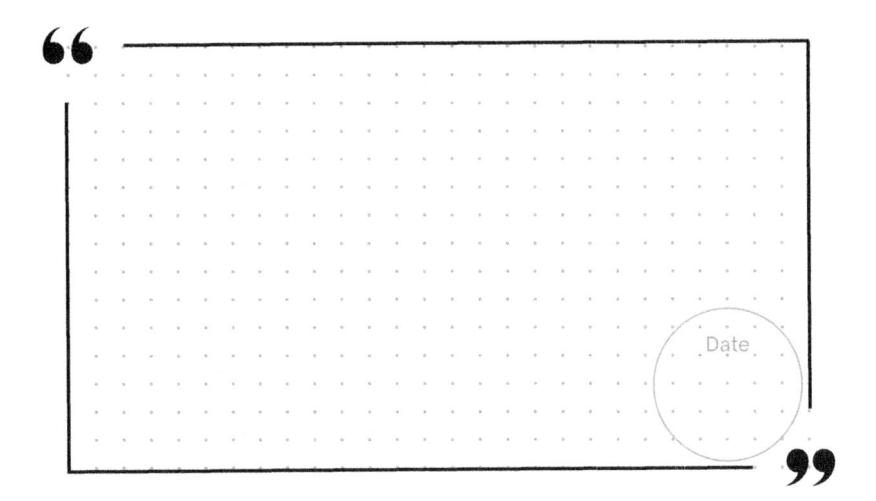

"

Date

"

Chapter 136

ONLY ACTION CURES FEAR

- **Act to Overcome:** Taking action is the way to overcome fear, not by waiting for fear to subside.
- **Confidence in Discomfort:** Confidence comes from being willing to face discomfort and take action despite it.
- **Fear's Shift:** Fear doesn't disappear but shifts to new challenges as you continue to act.

WHAT ACTION CAN I TAKE TODAY TO MOVE PAST MY CURRENT FEARS?

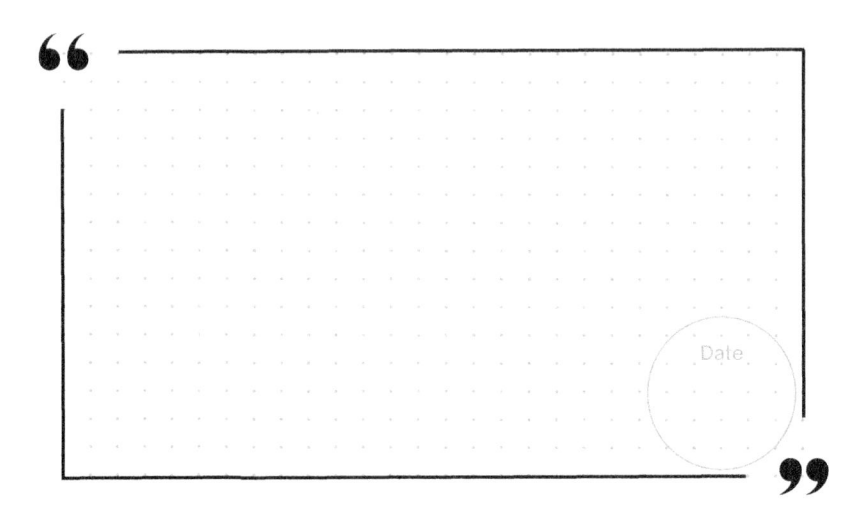

Date

Chapter 137

YOU'RE APOLOGIZING TOO MUCH

- **Shift Apologies:** Replace 'sorry' with phrases like 'thank you for waiting' or 'I'll fix that now.'
- **Be Assertive:** Use assertive language instead of apologizing for taking up space or asking for time.
- **Empower Yourself:** Recognize your own value and the power of your words.

HOW CAN I ADJUST MY LANGUAGE TO BE MORE ASSERTIVE AND LESS APOLOGETIC?

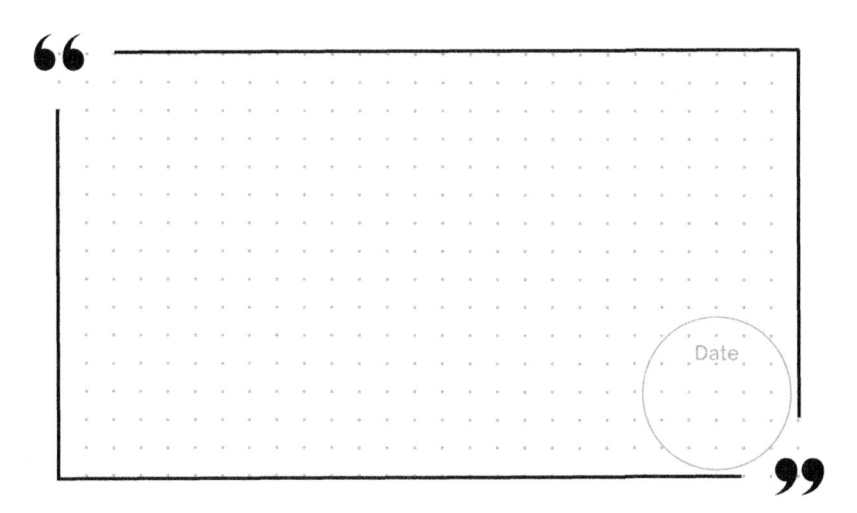

"
Date
"

Chapter 138

QUALIFICATIONS AREN'T EVERYTHING

- **Experience Over Credentials:** Prioritize practical experience over formal qualifications when seeking advice.
- **Action vs. Inaction:** Action and experience are critical for success; don't wait for perfect qualifications.
- **Self-Belief:** Believe in your potential and capabilities, regardless of formal qualifications.

HOW CAN I LEVERAGE MY EXPERIENCES AND ACTIONS RATHER THAN RELYING SOLELY ON FORMAL QUALIFICATIONS TO ACHIEVE MY GOALS?

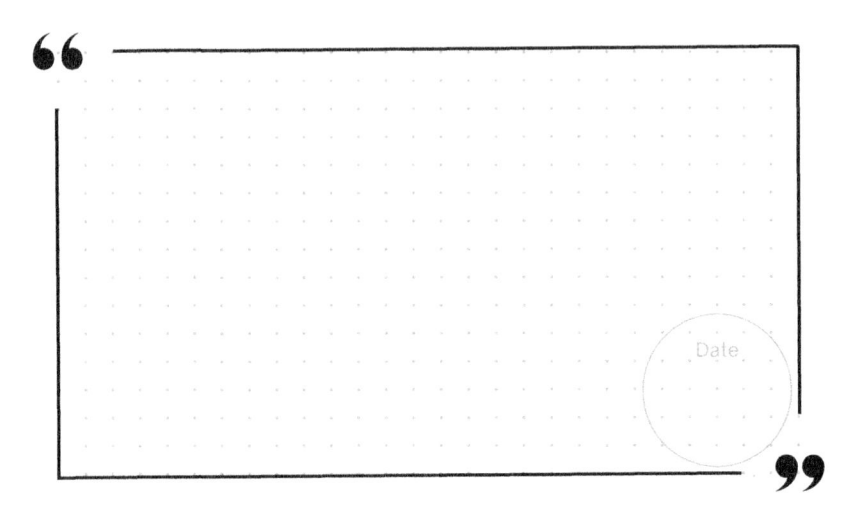

Date

Chapter 139

CLOSURE REQUIRES ONLY ONE PERSON

- **Self-Closure:** You don't need another person to find closure; you can decide to close the chapter yourself.
- **Avoid Gray Areas:** Clear decisions and boundaries help in moving forward and healing.
- **Emotional Wisdom:** Engage both the heart and mind to gain clarity and make decisive choices.

HOW CAN I FIND CLOSURE ON MY OWN, WITHOUT WAITING FOR EXTERNAL VALIDATION OR RESOLUTION FROM OTHERS?

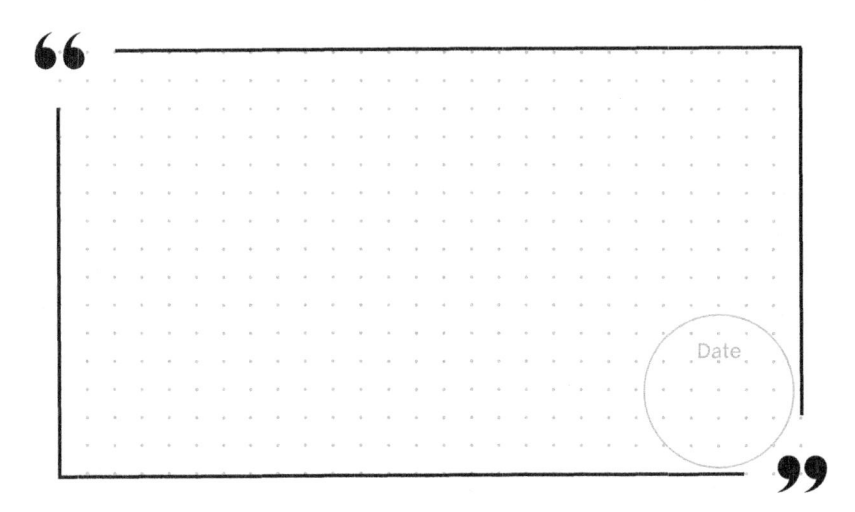

Date

Chapter 140

YOU DON'T HAVE TO FINISH WHAT YOU START

- **Prioritize Flexibility:** It's okay to drop projects or goals that no longer excite or serve you.
- **Trust Your Intuition:** Follow what genuinely interests you rather than feeling obligated to complete every start.
- **Relieve Pressure:** Allow yourself to let go of tasks or ambitions that no longer align with your current priorities.

DO I HAVE PROJECTS I COULD DROP IN ORDER TO MAKE MY LIFE EASIER?

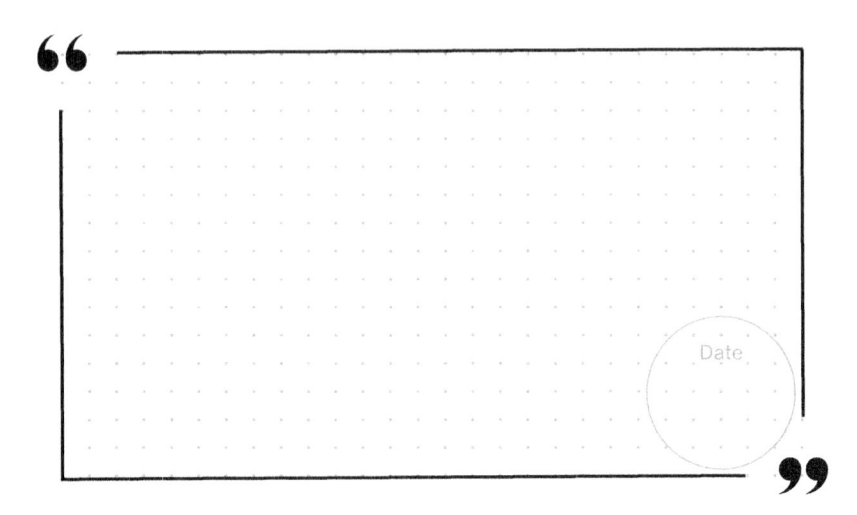

"

Date

"

Chapter 141

WHAT YOU DON'T LIKE IN SOMEONE ELSE, YOU PROBABLY DON'T LIKE IN YOURSELF

- **Self-Reflection:** Dislike or irritation towards others can reveal aspects of ourselves that we're struggling with.
- **Energy and Awareness:** Negative reactions to others often highlight unresolved issues or qualities we haven't fully embraced.
- **Mutual Reflection:** Positive admiration for others can also reflect qualities we possess within ourselves.

ARE THERE ASPECTS OF OTHERS THAT I DO NOT LIKE THAT MIGHT BE SOMETHING I CAN CHANGE IN MYSELF?

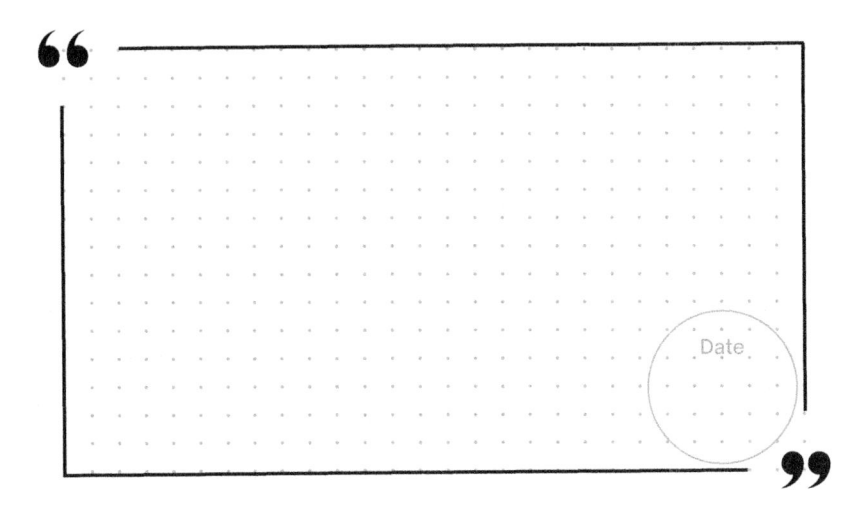

"

Date

"

Chapter 142

DOING IT IS EASIER THAN NOT DOING IT

- **Time Will Pass:** The time needed to pursue your dreams will pass regardless of whether you take action or not.
- **Act Now:** Embracing opportunities and desires now is easier than enduring dissatisfaction or unfulfilled dreams.
- **Avoid Regret:** Facing challenges and pursuing passions can prevent regret and create a more fulfilling life.

WHAT ACTION CAN I TAKE NOW TO START PURSUING MY DREAMS AND DESIRES, RATHER THAN WAITING FOR THE PERFECT MOMENT?

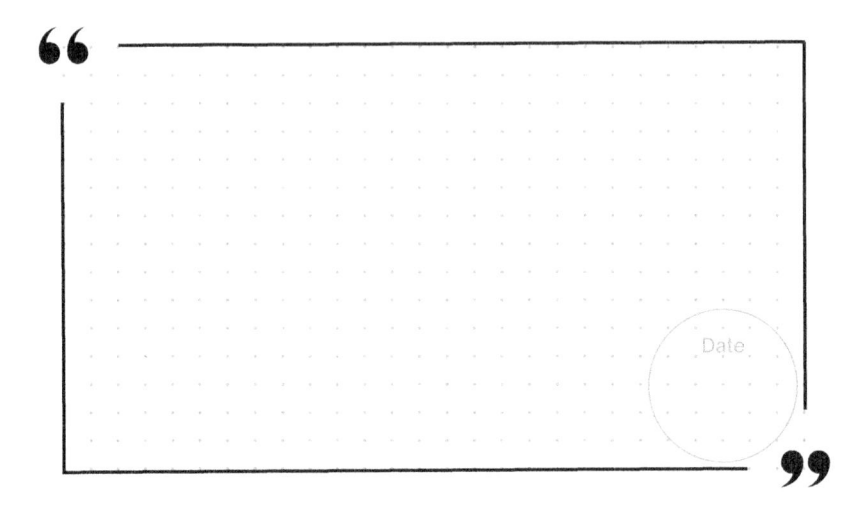

Chapter 143

BE A LIGHT FOR OTHERS

- **Lead by Example:** Show others that life can be simpler and more enjoyable by how you live.
- **Influence Through Action:** Inspire others through your actions and energy.
- **Generosity of Ease:** Demonstrate ease and joy to positively impact those around you.

HOW CAN I EMBODY MORE EASE IN MY LIFE TO POSITIVELY INFLUENCE THOSE AROUND ME AND CREATE A MORE JOYFUL ENVIRONMENT?

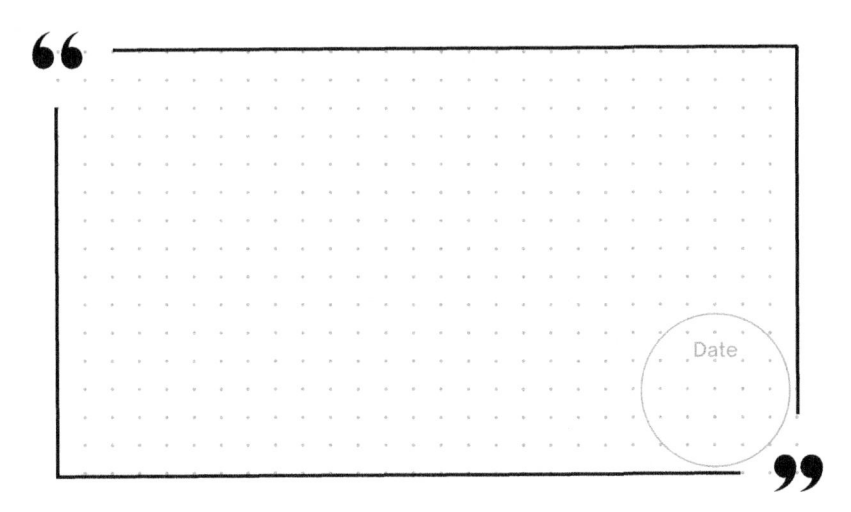

Journal

WHAT KEY LESSONS OR PRINCIPLES FROM THE BOOK WILL I CARRY WITH ME INTO THE FUTURE?

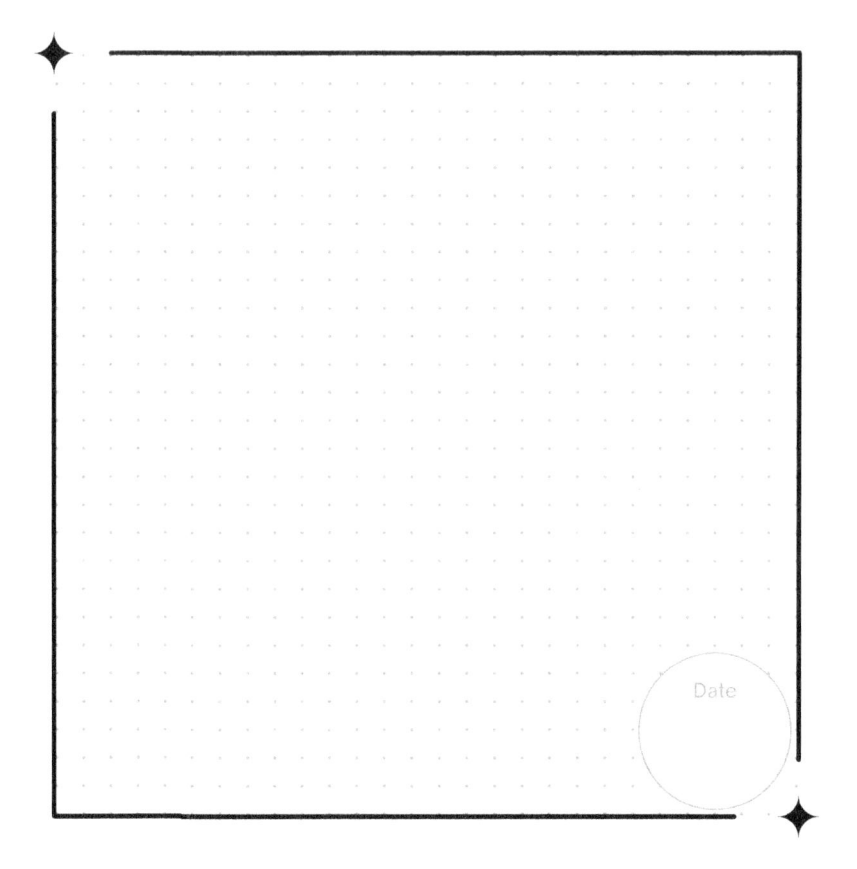

Date

Journal

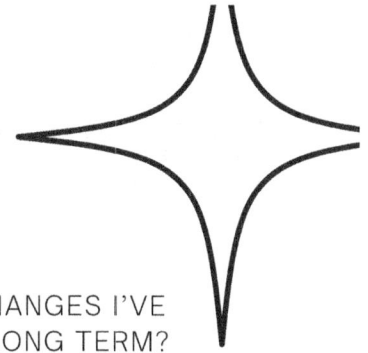

HOW CAN I ENSURE THAT THE CHANGES I'VE MADE ARE SUSTAINABLE IN THE LONG TERM?

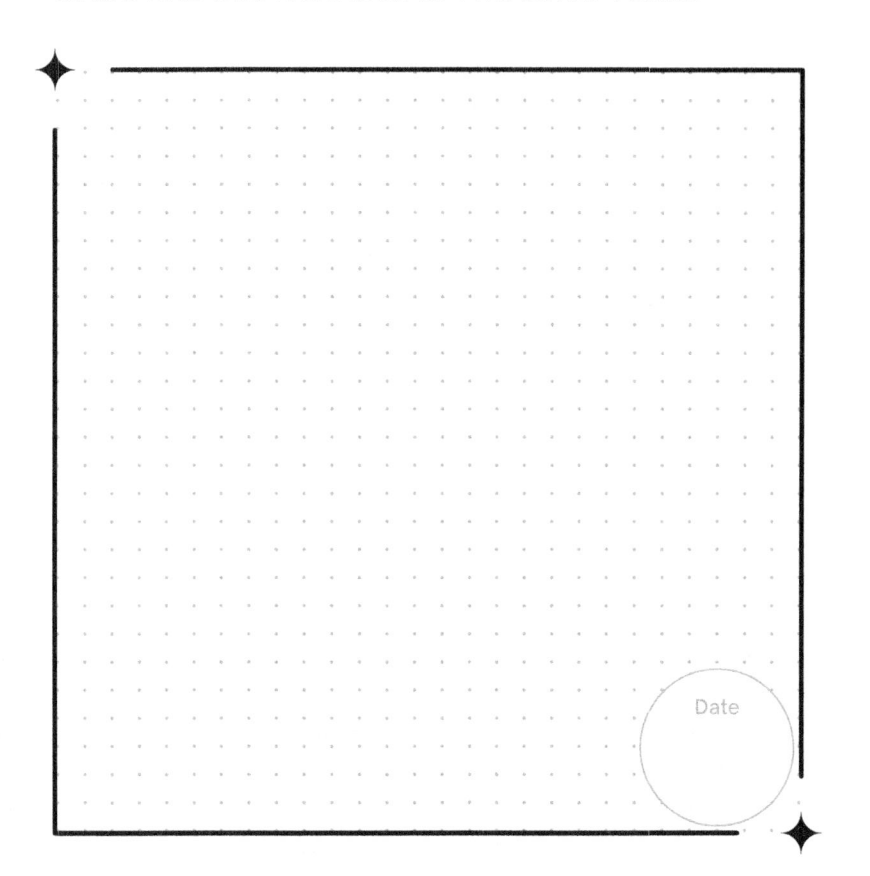

Date

Journal

HOW HAS THIS BOOK INSPIRED ME TO MAKE POSITIVE CHANGES?

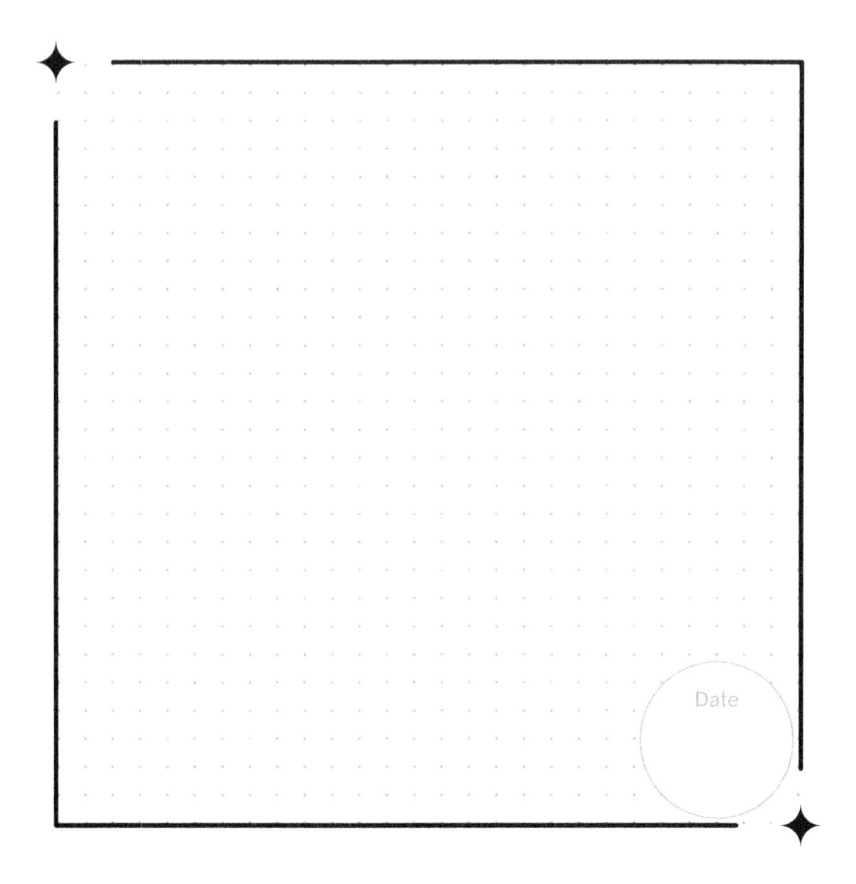

Date

Book Review

☆ ☆ ☆ ☆ ☆

USELESS: A waste of my time

OK BUT: It didn't make a big difference for me

DECENT READ: I got a few good takeaways from this book

GREAT HELP: Changed me and can be recommended to others

READ AGAIN: I can get even more out of this book

Date

How Can We Help?

I hope you enjoyed this book and that you gained more from "Let it be easy" by implementing its insights into your own life. If there are other books you'd like a workbook for, please don't hesitate to reach out to me.

Annie Agerbek
info@careclub.dk

PLEASE REVIEW

And finally: It would be a HUGE help to me, and I would be eternally grateful if you could review this workbook where you purchased it.

Thank you in advance.
With pleasure to serve, Annie

Printed in Great Britain
by Amazon